PLANET OF THE DOPES

Critics decry the "dumbing of America" while Beavis & Butt-head and Forrest Gump are superheroes in the American pop culture pantheon. Is stupidity contagious?

So it would seem. In *Dumb, Dumber, Dumbest*, John Kohut and Roland Sweet have compiled over 500 hilarious examples of human feeble-mindedness, including:

- The two elementary school janitors who tried to freeze a gopher with cleaning solvents and blew up the school instead. Nineteen people were hurt, but the gopher survived.

- The man who appeared in court to face charges of theft and probation violation and was arrested again, in the courtroom, for carrying a gym bag containing eighteen bags of marijuana.

Here is the first "dumb" book you'll ever love.

JOHN J. KOHUT is a political analyst for a large corporation in Washington, D.C. He has been collecting strange news clippings for over a decade and is the author of *Stupid Government Tricks*. **ROLAND SWEET** is a magazine editor and writes his own syndicated column. Kohut and Sweet co-authored *News from the Fringe*.

DUMB, DUMBER, DUMBEST

True News of the
World's Least
Competent People

Compiled by John J. Kohut
& Roland Sweet

A PLUME BOOK

PLUME

Published by the Penguin Group
Penguin Books USA Inc., 375 Hudson Street,
New York, New York 10014, U.S.A.
Penguin Books Ltd, 27 Wrights Lane, London W8 5TZ, England
Penguin Books Australia Ltd, Ringwood, Victoria, Australia
Penguin Books Canada Ltd, 10 Alcorn Avenue, Toronto,
Ontario, Canada M4V 3B2
Penguin Books (N.Z.) Ltd, 182–190 Wairau Road,
Auckland 10, New Zealand

Penguin Books Ltd, Registered Offices:
Harmondsworth, Middlesex, England

First published by Plume, an imprint of Dutton Signet,
a division of Penguin Books USA Inc.

First Printing, March, 1996
10

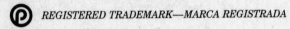 REGISTERED TRADEMARK—MARCA REGISTRADA

LIBRARY OF CONGRESS CATALOGING-IN-PUBLICATION DATA
Dumb, dumber, dumbest : true news of the world's least competent
people / compiled by John J. Kohut and Roland Sweet.
p.   cm.
ISBN 0-452-27595-4
1. Curiosities and wonders—Humor.   I. Kohut, John J.
II. Sweet, Roland.
PN6231.C85D86   1996

081—dc20

95–37810
CIP

Printed in the United States of America
Set in ITC Century Book

Designed by Jesse Cohen

Portions of this book first appeared in The National Enquirer.

For Shemp

Introduction

Stupid is as stupid does. Indeed! Leery of highbrows and smarty-pants, today's egalitarian-minded Americans revere Beavis & Butt-head, Ren and Stimpy, Wayne and Garth, *Dumb and Dumber* and other appeals to the lowest common denominator.

The *Baltimore Sun* decried this dumbing of American culture, lamenting the "wretched excess" of lowbrow. The "New Stupidity," the *New York Times* dubbed it. *Spy* magazine devoted seven pages to "Why It's Not So Smart to Be Smart Anymore," observing, "idiocy is being celebrated as something noble and pure."

Once, we extolled true heroes. Now we glorify screw-ups, misfits, and lunkheads.

Of whom there is no shortage. Kato Kaelin is just a drop in the bucket.

Why is nincompoopery so popular? Historian Richard Hofstadter noted in his study, *Anti-Intellectualism in American Life*, that dumbness is a recurring cycle in American history. H. L. Mencken warned that the "booboisie" were a force to be reckoned (but never reasoned) with. Voters scorned Adlai Stevenson because he was an egghead. They adored Dan Quayle because he wasn't—plus, he made George Bush look smart.

In his 1970 lowdown on lowbrows, *The Roob Revolution*, Roger Price quoted comedian Fred Allen. Asked where his audiences came from, Allen suggested, "There's a slow leak in Iowa."

Today, intellectual downplay is transcontinental. Global. Newspapers brim with examples.

Here's just one. Students representing Chicago's Steinmetz High School in a 1995 statewide academic decathlon finished first but were stripped of their title after the runners-up accused them of cheating. The second-place team's only evidence was the Steinmetz team's unusually high score on the day-long oral and written exams: 49,000 of a possible 60,000 points. The second school, which had won the previous nine competitions, charged that Steinmetz couldn't possibly have scored so high without cheating. That made sense to the Illinois Academic Decathlon Association. "You try to excel," Steinmetz team member Maciej Rupar, 17, said. "You do your best, and the people try to take it away for no reason."

Want more proof that mediocrity pays? Florida real estate investor Edward Seese left $4.5 million—30 percent of his fortune—to Broward Community College to fund 250 scholarships a year for *C* students. Seese's lawyer, Bill Leonard, explained that Seese didn't want average students to "be left out in the cold."

Such a climate made this book possible. It chronicles the most outrageous occurrences of shortsightedness, incompetence and poor judgment. Not just in the United States, but worldwide. Crooks and bureaucrats dominate.

Not all characters in these dispatches are stupid, we hasten to point out. Some are merely ridiculous or momentarily inept. Others are very bright people who became innocently entangled in improbable situations that turned out sounding stupid in newspaper accounts.

The papers that reported these occurrences are all reputable, mainstream bastions of journalism. As always, we dip our scissors in salute to the diligent reporters and sleeves-rolled-up editors who shepherded these strange stories into newsprint. Their efforts are responsible not just for the 500-plus items in this book, but also for the many others that we didn't have room for.

Perhaps you have clipped and saved an example or two of your favorite stupid human tricks. We would love to see copies. Send, with source and date, to:

Strange News
P.O. Box 25682
Washington, D.C. 20007

And now, dispatches from a strange planet.

I.
DUMB
HAPPENS

Hey, Moe!
Hey, Larry!

BRAZILIAN FARM WORKER FRANCISCO ASIS
dos Santos was so desperate to stop the pain from an
aching tooth that he put a pistol in his mouth and fired.
The *Globo* network reported that when Santos arrived
at the local hospital, doctors found that he had shot
out his eye, but the aching tooth remained.

WHILE HUNTING WITH A 17-YEAR-OLD
friend in Bloomfield, Indiana, Jack Constable, 18, shot
a squirrel, then decided to play a trick on his friend.
He hid behind a tree, picked up the squirrel and, hoping to attract his companion's attention, moved it
around as if it were running. The 17-year-old fell for

the ruse and fired his 12-gauge shotgun. The scatter shot wounded Constable in both hands, the left knee and the abdomen.

WHEN TWO MEN BROKE INTO HIS OFFICE in Milan, Italy, professional hypnotist Filadelfio Munafo, 39, put them in a trance—or so he thought until he told them to hand over their guns and they shot him. He explained later, "I was sure I had them in my power."

TO MEET THE JAPAN SUMO ASSOCIA-tion's minimum height requirement of 5-foot-8, 16-year-old aspirant Koji Harada had six inches of silicone implanted under his scalp, creating a large hairy lump atop his box-shaped head.

ROMANIAN PRISONERS BEGAN HAMMER-ing nails into their skulls to avoid hard labor. Inmates said they bang in the nails by hitting their heads on the wall, but guards insisted they use metal tea cups, according to Dr. Florin Vesa, head of the Galati County hospital. He noted that in just five months he operated on 17 inmates with nails in their head. "They only choose the rusty ones," he said, "and they put excrement on them."

 AFTER A WITNESS TOLD THE FREMONT County, Colorado, sheriff's office that he had seen a small plane plunge nose-first behind a hill, authorities launched a two-day air and ground search. According to Undersheriff Dale Rea, searchers were puzzled because they couldn't find the aircraft. Then a passing truck driver stopped at the searchers' command post and "told us he had also seen the aircraft go down, but he said it was just a big radio-controlled model airplane with about an eight-foot wingspan."

DONALD LEROY EVANS, 38, WHO WAS ACcused of strangling a Fort Lauderdale, Florida, prostitute, filed a motion before his trial to wear a Ku Klux Klan robe and for his name to be changed on all court documents to "the honorable and respected name of Hi Hitler." Courthouse employees explained that Evans thought Hitler's followers said "Hi, Hitler" rather than "*Heil*, Hitler."

Evans's misapprehension recalls the National Captioning Institute's discovery, just before sending off the final tape of the 1987 television movie *The Rise and Fall of the Third Reich*, that one of its editors had typed in for the crowd chant after every salute "Hi, Hitler!" instead of "*Heil*, Hitler!"

POLICE IN WESTPORT, CONNECTICUT, AR-rested Tracey and John O'Donnell after the couple got into a fight at their wedding reception. The bride told police that the disturbance began when her new husband fed her wedding cake too roughly after she told him to take it easy.

WHEN CAIRL D. COTHREN, 50, OF LA-bouchere Bay, Alaska, leaned over in the cab of his truck to spit tobacco juice into a can on the floor while holding a shotgun between his knees, he accidentally shot himself.

PROFESSIONAL HOUSE MOVERS DECIDED that the best route to move a 2,400-square-foot home belonging to Victor Bruce of Petoskey, Michigan, in

February was across frozen Walloon Lake. During the crossing, the wheeled undercarriage of I-beams that had been rigged beneath the house snagged on a three-inch bump in the ice, slowing the house enough that part of it broke through the ice.

IN POTTER COUNTY, TEXAS, THE FLAG OF

Chile flew over the courthouse for a whole day before Assistant District Attorney Paul Hermann asked why. Officials explained that the manufacturer had apparently put the similar Chilean flag in a package marked "Texas." Whoever opened the flag didn't notice the mistake either.

VERNON PIERCE, 33, SURRENDERED TO AU-

thorities in Glendale, Arizona, after a three-month marrying spree netted him four wives in two states. He said he told them that his job required him to travel, but that was a lie. "I didn't have a job," he explained. "I didn't have time." Besides having four wives, Pierce was dating other women. Police who searched his home found a list of women's names on a 3-by-5 card headed "Who to Marry."

AFTER A HOTEL WORKER IN VAXJO CITY,
Sweden, heard a voice calling for help inside a wall,
firefighters broke open a chimney pipe and found a
22-year-old man. He explained that nine hours earlier
he had one drink too many at the hotel bar, took a
walk on the hotel roof to clear his head and fell 45 feet
down the chimney.

AUTHORITIES IN WESTPORT, CONNECTICUT,
charged Halfdan Prahl, 35, with using a chain saw to
carve his initials into the barroom floor at the Viva
Zapata restaurant. Prahl explained that he thought the
restaurant was still owned by a man who he believed
would have found the stunt amusing.

IN 1994, A KOREAN AIR JETLINER CRASHED
in the southern resort of Cheju while landing during a
storm when the pilot and copilot argued whether the
runway was long enough, then fought each other for
control of the aircraft as it touched down, causing it
to skid off the runway and ram a safety barricade. All
152 passengers and eight crew members survived by
jumping down an escape chute moments before the
Airbus A300 exploded in flames. Pilot Barry Edward

Woods and copilot Chung Chankyu continued their argument, blaming each other for the crash.

TONY PERNER, 55, WAS CRITICALLY INjured when a small plane hit him on the runway of an airstrip in East Moriches, New York, while he was mooning the pilot. Pilot Frederick Spadaro told police that he didn't see Perner while taking off because it was getting dark.

AFTER COMPLAINTS OF A PLANE FLYING erratically and buzzing houses in Leesburg, Florida, a Lake County sheriff's deputy met the plane at the airport. The three passengers were nude, and pilot Phillip C. Smith, 49, had his shirt off and his pants half off. Smith explained that taking off their clothes just seemed like a good idea.

EDO RANKEN, 91, OF SYRACUSE, NEbraska, was waiting to take a driving test to have his license renewed when he decided to make sure his reverse gear was working. He backed out of the parking space near the courthouse, but when he tried to pull back in he stepped on the brake and the gas pedal at the same time. The car jumped the curb, climbed a muddy, snow-covered bank, knocked over a 3,000-pound Ten Commandments monument and pushed it about 6 feet. The car then crossed a street and hit a parked van. Ranken, who suffered minor injuries, said that he had a perfect driving record since 1917 and wasn't going to let the fact that he plowed into the Ten Commandments stop him from taking his driver's test, just as soon as his car was fixed.

AFTER THREE MEMBERS OF PEOPLE UN-limited, a group that believes its members can live forever simply by wishing it, died, spokesperson Beryl Gregory defended the group's credibility by explaining that the three deceased members hadn't lived forever because they didn't believe hard enough.

IN ST. JAMES, MINNESOTA, DAIRY FARMER Herbert Saunders, 64, was charged with swindling terminally ill people by injecting his cows with their blood and selling them the cows' milk, explaining that the "antibodies" in the milk could cure cancer, AIDS and diabetes. Watonwan County authorities said people

were paying $35 a bottle for milk, then Saunders got
them to buy whole cows for $2,500 each.

MEN IN IVANO-FRANKIVSK, UKRAINE, WHO
couldn't resist buying newly arrived Syrian-made
shoes, reported several days later that the soles began
peeling away, the colors ran and the new shoes quickly
fell apart. Local investigators discovered that the styl-
ish footwear, imported and sold off at a handsome
profit by a small private company, was intended to be
worn by corpses at Syrian funerals.

FOUR POLICE OFFICERS IN WAUKEGAN, IL-
linois, were injured during a six-hour class designed to
teach police officers how to reduce injuries while sub-
duing offenders. According to Police Chief Phillip Stevenson, three of the men suffered their injuries at the
hands of other officers. The fourth broke his toe while
stumbling on foam mats that were used to pad the
floor.

EMERGENCY PHONE LINES WERE ALL TIED up in Malaysia by thousands of calls after word spread that people could contact dead spirits by dialing the numbers 999998, 999444 and 999999. All such attempted calls were immediately connected to the 999 number for police, fire and ambulance emergencies. Those working the emergency phone lines said that when they picked up, the people on the other end thought they had made contact with the dead and immediately began chanting incantations, asking questions about what life was like in heaven or hell and asking for winning lottery numbers.

JAMES SCOTT, 24, OF FOWLER, ILLINOIS, was sentenced to life in prison for sabotaging a levee on the Mississippi River during a 1993 flood. Noting that the breach submerged 14,000 acres of farmland, prosecutors said Scott told friends that he moved some sandbags to flood an area so that his wife could not return from her job on the Missouri side because he wanted to "have affairs" and "party."

A 24-YEAR-OLD GARFIELD, NEW JERSEY, man died when he ran over himself. According to Bergen County Prosecutor John Fahy, the unidentified man, who had been drinking heavily, apparently began vomiting in his car and placed the automatic transmission into what he thought was park. It was actually reverse, Fahy said, and as the driver opened the door, he fell out and rolled under the front wheel, which pinned his neck, suffocating him.

. . . .

TO TEST THE STEREOTYPE OF GERMAN willingness to obey orders, students at the University of Trier in the Rhineland-Palatinate put signs on two phone booths near campus. One said MEN ONLY and the other WOMEN ONLY. Of the 69 people observed using the phones, almost all the women and 75 percent of the men obeyed the signs.

. . . .

TO WARN THE PUBLIC ABOUT FOURTH OF July brush fires, sheriff's deputies and firefighters gathered at a remote bomb-disposal range outside San Diego to blow up thousands of illegal fireworks for the news media. Sparks from the demonstration fell onto a nearby hill, causing a 10-acre brush fire that required 50 firefighters, two water-dropping helicopters and a bulldozer to extinguish.

An ABC News–Washington Post poll

found that 52 percent of those surveyed would rather spend a week in jail than be president. Most black, male, younger and middle-class people would choose the presidency, while most female, white, older and working-class individuals said they would prefer jail.

In Bembridge, England, on the Isle

of Wight, Daniel Arthure, 20, was so absorbed by rock music he was listening to on his headphones that he didn't hear a Cessna 150 aircraft crash-land on the lawn of his home or the frantic rescue of its two injured passengers. Arthure said the first he knew something was wrong was when he looked out his kitchen window as fire engines and police cars pulled up outside and saw "dozens of people running 'round my garden."

The state-run Zimbabwe Broadcast-

ing Corporation issued a three-month suspension to two television news announcers who burst out laughing during the news. Officials said that co-anchors Tsitsi Vera and Noreen Welch "lost their composure" when reading a report about a woman who gave birth in the bathroom of a train. The baby fell through the toilet onto the track but survived.

....

THE DAY AFTER AN ARMY SERGEANT STA-
tioned in Maryland won a court order legally changing his name to Jesus Christ Hallelujah, he announced that he was petitioning the Anne Arundel Circuit Court to change his name back to Tyrone Victor Wright. He said he made the decision after talking it over with his family, explaining, "We're all happy with Tyrone Victor Wright."

....

DAVID GRACEY, 51, TRIED TO KILL HIMSELF
by inhaling natural gas after unhooking a pipe in the basement of his house in Greeley, Colorado. The gas ignited, causing an explosion that leveled his single-family house. The blast also injured him, his wife and a neighbor, and damaged several other houses on the block. Damages totaled $1.3 million. "I thought that method was fail-safe," Gracey said. "Remember the stories of people sticking their head in the oven? I've learned since that natural gas isn't poisonous."

AFTER COMPLAINTS FROM HIS NEIGH-
bors, town selectmen in Peru, Vermont, ordered Ronald Williams to stop feeding dog food, cereal and soft
drinks to hundreds of rats on his property. The town
temporarily evicted Williams, giving him $700 for lodg-
ing, while exterminators were called in to kill the rats.
Town officials also ordered him not to resume his rat
feedings upon his return home.

AFTER A MAN NEAR HARRISBURG, PENN-
sylvania, decided to use a shop vacuum to siphon gasoline from the car he was preparing to trade in, a spark
from the vacuum ignited the gas, sending flames 30
feet into the air. The resulting fire destroyed the car
and the man's newly renovated $200,000 home.

ALERTED BY A STUDENT AT FOWLER EL-
ementary School in Ceres, California, that a gopher
was in the building, three janitors cornered the animal
in a utility room. Jeff Davis, 35, explained that he and
his colleagues proceeded to spray the rodent with several canisters of a solvent used to remove gum from
floors, hoping "to freeze it to death." As one janitor
lighted a cigarette in the poorly ventilated room,

sparks from the lighter ignited the solvent. The ensuing explosion blew all three out of the room and injured 16 students. The gopher survived the encounter and was released in a field.

A MISSILE FIRED BY A RUSSIAN ATTACK jet during an exercise went astray and narrowly missed striking a nuclear power plant and an apartment complex. "We have repeatedly asked that the missile testing range be moved," the regional governor complained, "but the answer was always negative."

DESPITE SUFFERING A STROKE AFTER eating 38 eggs in 29 seconds before an audience that, fortunately, included an emergency medical technician, American Mort Hurst, 44, announced four years later that he would appear on a Madrid television show to down a dozen eggs as quickly as possible.

TAIWANESE HEALTH AUTHORITIES FINED Hsiao Ming Hospital $12,200 and barred it from accepting patients for two weeks after one of its surgeons mistakenly removed the appendixes of 11 children who were simply suffering from a case of food poisoning.

POLICE IN SPRINGFIELD, MASSACHU-setts, said that the man they arrested for chopping at that city's famed bronze statue, *The Puritan*, with a hatchet, was under the false impression that it was made out of copper, which he was hoping to sell for scrap.

A FEDERAL DRUG RAID AT A WASHING-ton, D.C., public housing complex involving more than 200 federal agents and city police officers had to be canceled at the last minute because the city housing agency issued a press release the night before announcing the sweep. The agent in charge of the operation was driving to the staging area that morning when he heard news on the radio of the supposedly secret operation, which had been six months in the planning and cost hundreds of thousands of dollars. A spokesperson for the housing agency insisted that the mistake "in no way diminishes our commitment to assist law enforcement agencies."

POLICE HAD TO BREAK UP A FIGHT BE-
tween 30 to 40 people on an Ohio university campus
after a group of black men confronted a group of white
men dressed up for a Halloween party. The blacks mistakenly believed that the whites, actually costumed as
the pope and his entourage, were dressed as members
of a white supremacist group.

Read the Instructions

WHEN HIS CAR'S FUEL LINE FROZE, George Gibbs, 23, of Columbus, Ohio, figured the solution was to heat up some gasoline on his stove. Fumes from the two-gallon can ignited, however, singeing Gibbs's face and hair. He tried to smother the fire by throwing a blanket over the stove, but doing so caused flames to spread to his kitchen ceiling and into his living room. He decided the time had come to call firefighters, who extinguished the blaze.

A 44-YEAR-OLD WISCONSIN MAN TRIED TO kill himself with an overdose of nicotine. The *Journal of the American Medical Association* reported that after consuming a pot of coffee, the man stuck seven nicotine patches on his chest and began smoking cigarettes two at a time, hoping to cause a heart attack. Two hours later, he changed his mind and tore off the patches.

IN NEW ORLEANS, AN EXPLOSION THAT injured two people and wrecked the French Quarter apartment where Tennessee Williams wrote *A Streetcar Named Desire* was caused by flames from a water heater igniting the insecticide spray from six "roach bombs." The blast blew out windows and the kitchen ceiling and buckled the apartment's floor and walls. It also blew the front door off the three-story building onto a passerby. Firefighter Norman Woodridge said that Cheron Brylski, who had just rented the apartment, set off the aerosol cans of insecticide in the 8-by-10-foot kitchen. The recommended treatment is one can for a 20-by-30-foot room.

ROMANIANS FLORIAN IORGA, 42, AND HIS son Aurel, 16, were electrocuted by the booby trap they had set up outside their home in Bucharest to protect their onion patch. They heard noises in the night and ran out to investigate, only to trip over the cables wired to the mains.

IN THE RUSSIAN TOWN OF TULA, A 25-year-old poacher put a live electrical cable into a pond to catch fish. Authorities reported that he forgot to disconnect the wire before getting into the water to collect the fish and was electrocuted.

IN CORPUS CHRISTI, TEXAS, WILLIAM Chadwick, 31, died while pretending to hang himself as a stunt for a haunted house party after the rope he rigged up malfunctioned.

A 32-YEAR-OLD MAN WAS KILLED ON Washington's Capital Beltway when his car rammed into a truck stopped on the shoulder. Virginia state police spokesperson Lucy Caldwell said the man may have lost control of his car on the busy high-speed highway while he was eating a salad.

AUTHORITIES INVESTIGATING A FIRE THAT ignited 1,700 tons of ammunition at an arms depot outside Bolshoi Kamen, Russia, said the blaze was caused by an off-duty guard who tried to dismantle a sophisticated missile component with a pocket knife.

AFTER WATCHING A TELEVISION SHOW about suicide facilitator Dr. Jack Kevorkian, John Campbell, 51, a cancer patient in Mankato, Minnesota, tried to kill himself by turning on a gas oven. Instead, he caused an explosion that destroyed part of his apartment house and temporarily displaced seven people. Avis Woehrle, the building's owner, said that Campbell came downstairs after the explosion and told her, "I'm on fire. I tried to kill myself. Call the fire department."

IN OCTOBER 1993, AIR FORCE PILOT LIEUT. Col. Don Snelgrove lost control of his F-16C fighter jet when he set the aircraft on automatic pilot and undid the lap belt to urinate into his "piddle pack," a dehydrated sponge in a plastic container. According to the *Stars and Stripes* newspaper, the belt's buckle got wedged between the ejection seat and the control stick. As Snelgrove adjusted the seat, the control stick shifted to the right, causing the jet to plunge from 33,000 feet to 2,000 feet. Unable to regain control, Snelgrove ejected, and the $18 million fighter jet crashed in Turkey.

A SIMILAR INCIDENT OCCURRED IN DECEMber 1990. Air Force Cpt. Craig Fisher crashed his F-16 jet near Palmdale, California, after he had to urinate during the flight. He told investigators that he put the aircraft on automatic pilot and took a plastic pouch from a pocket in his flight suit. As he pressed on the rudder pedals to help raise himself to go, the plane began to roll and dive. He immediately sat down but was unable to right the plane and bailed out.

IN GLENWOOD SPRINGS, COLORADO, A plumber working court-ordered community service hours in a state fish hatchery accidentally killed 122,000 Colorado River cutthroat trout when he turned the wrong valve and sent hot water flowing into an incubator.

WHEN A 45-YEAR-OLD MAN IN LONG ISland, New York, failed to defrost frozen pipes in his home using a blow torch, he decided to back his 1984

Buick up against the house and let the car exhaust flow into the crawl space and do the trick. He, his wife and three children were all hospitalized for carbon monoxide poisoning.

WHEN A COLORADO JUDGE PRESIDING over a murder trial declared John Peters, Jr., an expert witness in aerosol chemical sprays and self-defense, the prosecutor handed Peters an aerosol bear repellent device for his examination. Peters was demonstrating how to hold the can of Bear-Guard when he hit the trigger twice, sending a spray directly at the prosecutor. As the noxious odor spread, people ran coughing from the courtroom. After the trial reconvened in another room an hour later, the judge ordered Peters's testimony stricken from the record.

A 46-YEAR-OLD KENTUCKY MAN AND HIS 15-year-old nephew were electrocuted when they tried to restore electricity to a nearby house by taking a 50-foot television antenna and inserting it into an electrical transformer on a utility pole.

Mensa Rejects

CANADIAN AMBULANCE DRIVER ARTHUR Russell had to be rescued just six hours after he set out to row across the Atlantic Ocean in a homemade boat. Russell's only experience at sea had been one time when he rode on a ferry, although he had practiced for his maiden voyage for two years, using a rowing machine in his house.

IN DENVER, MARILYN ANDERSON, 47, shot herself while trying to stop her 10 dogs from fighting. She told police that she routinely fired at the ceiling to quiet her pets. The noise usually worked, she explained, but this time it didn't. When she went to clear the weapon, she forgot that she had put a bullet in the gun and shot herself in the hand.

CHRISTOPHER BLEDSOE, 26, SHOT HIM-self while destroying the family cat. He said he was holding the cat in one hand and a .22-caliber pistol in the other. He fired. The bullet passed through the cat and pierced Bledsoe's finger.

IN ENGLAND, BARRY MOULSDALE WAS walking along a 24,000-volt overhead railway line as if it were a tightrope when he fell. His friend Robert Woolf told police investigating the incident, "My mate's father did this some time ago and he had his arm blown off, so we thought we'd try it."

AT A RICHLAND COUNTY, SOUTH CARO-lina, trial concerning obscenity standards, two male police officers took to the floor of the courtroom to demonstrate dancing techniques used by the nude dancing women of the Chippen-Dolls nightclub. The two proceeded to wrap their legs around a microphone stand and then got down on all fours and shook their butts at the jury. As the courtroom erupted in laughter, the prosecutor begged the jury to ignore the humor in the case.

EXPLAINING HIS CAR CRASH TO A MUNICH court, a motorist said that he took his hands off the wheel because, "I wanted to know, so I let go and asked: 'God, can you drive?'"

IN 1982 THE MARYLAND POISON CENTER reported that nearly 80 people had been poisoned in two months after mistaking the new Lever Brothers Company dishwashing liquid Sun Light for lemon juice and adding it to iced tea and other drinks. The product's label proclaimed that it contained "real lemon juice."

IN 1993, EMMETT "SKIP" DYE, 55, walked 3,155 miles across the country from Ocean City, Maryland, to the California coastline in 189 days, going west by walking eastward. Shuttling two cars by himself, Dye would drive one car a few miles west, park it and walk back to get the other car. Then he would drive the second car a few miles past the first and repeat the process.

IN THE PHILIPPINES, ROGELIO APARICIO, 46, despondent after his wife left him, shot himself in the temple, but the bullet only grazed his head. The Philippine News Agency reported that Aparicio then aimed the revolver in his mouth but again missed, grazing only his lips. After his second failure, police arrested him for using an unlicensed gun.

ALFREDO ROSALES, 32, OF BUENOS Aires, died in a hospital intensive care unit after eating a whole piglet for dinner. The family of the 660-pound man explained that his eating had gotten out of hand.

IN HOUSTON, SERVANDO C. RODRIGUEZ, 27, complained of back pain until his uncle, a "witch doctor," suggested a treatment to "exorcise the pain," according to Harris County Sheriff's Sgt. John Den-

holm. The treatment called for placing cotton sprin-
kled with rubbing alcohol in a jar, igniting it and turning the jar upside down on the man's back. The flames
would die out from lack of oxygen, and the resulting
vacuum would draw out the pain.

Denholm said that for some reason the uncle
couldn't perform the procedure and had his landlord's
wife do it. When the woman began rubbing alcohol on
Rodriguez's back, it caught fire from the cigarette in
her mouth, causing her to jump up and spill alcohol in
her lap, which also ignited. Rodriguez died from burns
to his back and groin.

SOCCER FANS IN A BOLIVIAN VILLAGE
were so busy celebrating their national team's win over
Uruguay that they failed to notice their houses were
on fire. Firecrackers thrown by revelers fell onto the
thatched roofs, setting fire to 40 houses, almost the
entire village of Ixiamas, according to regional prefect
Adolfo Soliz, who said all of them burned to the
ground.

IN FLORIDA, A DELTA AIRLINES JETLINER
carrying 42 passengers to Palm Beach International
Airport tried for 39 minutes to contact the control
tower, then had to land without guidance or clearance.

Investigators discovered the lone air traffic controller on duty was taking a nap, according to Federal Aviation Administration spokesperson Anne Eldridge, who explained, "This is hardly a good situation."

BRITISH CIVIL SERVANT ROY WHITE, 43, committed suicide by attaching a hose to his car's exhaust after a hair transplant and other remedies failed to cure his baldness. His wife, Linda, told an inquest in the town of Hitchin that her husband could not sleep at night for worrying about his thinning hair. "He fell into a depression totally associated with the fact he was going bald," she explained. "He talked continually about his baldness."

DURING THE TRIAL OF CLEOPHUS "LITTLE Pie" Prince, Jr., 26, charged with murdering six women, the prosecutor showed the jury a videotape of one of the victims, an aspiring actress, to emphasize the tragedy of her death. Among the people in the courtroom overcome by emotion while watching the tape was Prince's attorney, whose sobbing prompted the judge to call a recess. The jury ultimately sentenced Prince to be executed.

IN BANGKOK, GOVERNMENT WORKER Somjet Korkeaw, 42, was about to leave work at 3 o'clock Saturday afternoon when he realized he had left some belongings on a floor above. Since passenger elevators had been turned off by then, Somjet squeezed into a small cargo elevator designed to carry food and documents between floors. His 150 pounds were more than the elevator was designed to lift, and it stopped between floors. Somjet spent 40 hours in the one-cubic-yard space before the office reopened Monday morning and a maintenance worker rescued him.

BUNGEE JUMPER WILLIAM BROTHERTON, 20, leapt from a hot air balloon tethered over a field in Arvada, Colorado, but he had incorrectly figured the length of the cord and made it 70 feet too long. He died on impact.

THREE TEXAS NATIONAL GUARDSMEN were shot to death during night vision training by fellow soldiers who apparently mistook the victims for pop-up targets being used in the exercise.

FOUR MEN WHO ACCEPTED A $15,000 challenge from British animal rights activist Rebecca Hall to live like hens in a cold, cramped cage for a week lasted just 18 hours. The cage, which had no sanitation facilities, measured three feet square and just over six feet high, duplicating what Hall called "animal concentration camps" used to produce cheap chickens. Richard Brett, one of the four men who failed the challenge, said, "I feel stiff, sore and knackered [worn out], and was not enormously disappointed when they unlocked the door."

YU-TE CHEN, A TAIWANESE CITIZEN, WAS apprehended as he was about to board a plane at Los Angeles International Airport. Chen was carrying 18 snakes wrapped in nylon sacks and strapped to his biceps and 34 other snakes in a brown paper bag. He was sentenced to a month in prison for smuggling protected reptiles.

WHEN A CUSTOMS SERVICE AGENT IN MI-ami searched the luggage of Manuel Frade, 20, on arrival from Venezuela, she touched a pair of jeans and felt something wriggling. It turned out to be 14 juvenile boa constrictors. A further search of Frade's bags found hundreds of tarantulas, their eggs and 300 poison-arrow frogs, all smuggled in violation of the Endangered Species Act.

AUTHORITIES AT BALTIMORE–WASHINGton International Airport arrested Robert A. Daverio for smuggling more than 250 tortoises and turtles in his suitcase.

AUTHORITIES AT SPAIN'S MADRID–Barajas Airport arrested Francisco Javier Gibert, 29, when a security check found him carrying a live baby crocodile and a baby caiman alligator attached to small wooden planks inside the lining of his jacket.

A MINISTER IN ENFIELD, NEW HAMPshire, who started buying guns because he feared the Brady Law would infringe on his rights, accidentally shot himself to death while demonstrating gun safety to his family. Police said that Herbert Kershaw, 59, minister of the New Life Christian Fellowship Church, began buying guns after passage of the federal law requiring a waiting period before handgun purchases. He attended a firearms course and later that day was pointing out a .45-caliber pistol's safety features, not realizing the gun was loaded, when it went off.

....

THE MOST WANTED TERRORIST IN THE world, Illich Ramirez Sanchez, alias Carlos the Jackal, eluded authorities for more than 20 years. He was finally caught when he emerged from hiding in Sudan and checked into a hospital in Khartoum to undergo liposuction to remove fat from around his waist. *The Observer*, a British newspaper, quoted a Sudanese doctor in Cairo who said that as soon as Carlos was unconscious from the anesthetic for the cosmetic procedure, French agents seized him.

....

DURING A PROFESSIONAL WRESTLING match in Ludhiana, India, combatants Ultimate Warrior and Mr. Demolition Ax hurled two chairs at the audience, injuring two men and three children. When the fighters shouted the usual insults at the audience, two local wrestlers, Kehar Singh and Sumer Singh, jumped into the ring and punched the Americans.

Unaware that the Indian wrestlers were part of the act, several youths joined them in the ring and beat up the American wrestlers with field hockey sticks. Police broke up the fight and ended the match. Ultimate Warrior, Mr. Demolition Ax and one spectator were hospitalized.

IN TRACY, CALIFORNIA, GASTON LYLE

Senac, 20, accidentally killed himself by showing his friends how rock star Kurt Cobain shot himself in the head with a shotgun. According to police Sgt. Jim Hanson, Senac propped a shotgun on the floor and knelt with his mouth over the barrel. "He wasn't intending to hurt himself," Hanson explained. "He put the gun up to his head and said, 'Look, I'm just like Kurt Cobain,' and the gun went off."

MANY OF THE 67 OREGON CONVICTS WHO

volunteered to have the government bombard their testicles with radiation did it for the money, according to the federal Department of Energy. Between 1963 and 1973, inmates received $5 a month for exposing their scrotum and testes to X rays and for providing samples of urine, blood and semen. They got $10 for each biopsy of the testicles.

POLICE AND PARAMEDICS IN LAKELAND, Florida, rescued a 33-year-old man trapped in a motel swimming pool. They reported that "his pants were down to his knees and his penis was stuck in a suction hole." Paramedics inserted a lubricant around the suction fitting, and after about forty minutes were able to free him.

IN SOMERVILLE, NEW JERSEY, SHERIFF'S cadet Robert Langenbech was suspended for three days without pay after officials said he used a disguised dummy to stand guard in his place at the Somerset County courthouse while he took a nap.

IN BURLINGTON, WISCONSIN, MICHAEL Webber, 24, known for being able to hold his breath for a long period of time, was demonstrating his ability in a pool, police said, when he died of a heart attack.

MAGDALENA JAWORSKA, 33, WHO WAS
Miss Poland of 1984 and competed in that year's Miss
World competition, died in 1994 while taking a bath
when she dropped an electric hair dryer into the water.

LIEUT. COL. JULIO RAMON RIVERA, 47, A
U.S. serviceman in El Salvador, went to a police barracks to press for the release of three Salvadoran employees of the American Embassy, who had been
detained for drinking and carrying weapons, including
a hand grenade. Rivera tried to prove that the weapons
were fake by pulling the pin on the grenade. It exploded, killing him, two Salvadoran police officers and
two of the arrested employees.

AN 18-YEAR-OLD MAN IN RIVERSIDE, CAL-
ifornia, was using a semiautomatic pistol while imitat-
ing a gangsta rap act he saw on television when he
accidentally shot himself in the mouth.

FEDERAL SAFETY OFFICIALS INVESTIGAT-ing why an American Airlines jumbo jet went into a 16-second nosedive that injured 17 passengers and crew members blamed the incident on a pilot search-ing for a place to put a box of soft drinks and coffee. A spokesperson for the National Transportation Safety Board said that the flight from Miami to Buenos Aires was over Jamaica when a flight attendant brought the drinks to the cockpit.

Trying to be helpful, the reserve first officer reached over and slid the first officer's seat forward to make room for the drinks behind it. The movement startled the first officer and pushed his legs into the control column, disengaging the auto pilot and causing the nosedive. In addition to the injuries, which resulted from passengers and crew being thrown about the cabin, much of the food that was being served at the time wound up plastered on the ceiling.

AUTHORITIES INVESTIGATING THE CRASH of a Russian airliner that killed all 75 aboard blamed the mishap on the captain, Yuroslav Kudrinsky, who was giving flying lessons to his two children in the cockpit. A transcript of the in-flight recorder showed Kudrinsky, copilot Igor Peskaryov, Kudrinsky's 12-year-old daughter Yana and his 16-year-old son Eldar were in the cockpit.

Kudrinsky gave up his seat first to Yana, then to

Eldar, who turned the wheel, shutting off the automatic pilot and sending the aircraft into a dive. As the captain and copilot yelled to Eldar to turn the other way, the boy struggled to get out of the captain's seat.

Captain: Get out.

Copilot: There's the ground.

Captain: Crawl out to the back. Get out! Get out!
*   Get out! Get out! Get out! Get out! Get out!*
*   Get out! Get out! Get out! Get out! Get out!*

Then, according to state air-safety investigator Vsevolod Ovcharov, the boy's foot "accidentally pushed the right pedal, sending the aircraft into a spin. . . . The situation became irreversible."

AN AEROFLOT CHARTER PLANE CRASHED near Baku, the capital of Azerbaijan, in 1995 after it ran out of fuel. An inspector at the crash site said the crew apparently forgot to refuel the plane at its previous stop.

IN PLACER COUNTY, CALIFORNIA, REUBEN Warnes, 19, swung off the 728-foot-high Foresthill Bridge tethered to a 115-foot rope, but when he tried to climb the rope back to the bridge, ice crystals that had formed on it prevented the climb. He dangled for more than three hours in the frigid morning air until rescuers arrived and hoisted him back up to the bridge. Authorities said Warnes would be billed for the cost of emergency equipment and personnel summoned to the scene from seven local and state agencies.

....

WHILE DAVID WAYNE GODIN, 22, WAS RE-turning home from his bachelor party in Dartmouth, Nova Scotia, his vehicle plunged into a lake. He drowned after being unable to swim to the surface because of the weight of a ball and chain attached to his leg by his friends at the party.

....

TAMARA JO KLEMKOWSKY, 32, OF WAL-dorf, Maryland, was returning from a bachelorette party aboard a chartered bus when she tried to moon a passing car. Maryland State Trooper Kim Brooks noted the bus was traveling 55 mph when Klemkowsky leaned against an emergency window, which gave way, sending her tumbling onto the highway.

IN DENVER, AN ARGUMENT OVER WHERE to eat Christmas Eve dinner prompted Celeste De-Herrera, 27, to set a fire that killed a house guest, according to arson investigator Leon Beesley. He testified that after arguing with her boyfriend, Ronnie Gonzalez, DeHerrera set fire to Gonzalez's presents—pants and a shirt—then went to the bedroom and threw the clothes at Gonzalez. Beesley said the woman then ignited the family Christmas tree and warned Gonzalez and his two children, "Get ready to die." The ensuing blaze killed house guest Leroy Mitchell, 29.

A LOS ANGELES COUNTY PARKING CON-trol officer ticketed a Cadillac that was illegally parked next to a curb on street-sweeping day, even though the driver was sitting behind the wheel. The driver didn't protest or offer any excuses when the meter man reached inside the car to leave the ticket on the dashboard because he was dead, having been shot in the head.

Paramedics who arrived at the scene after residents reported the body said it was difficult to imagine how the parking officer could have left the $30 citation without noticing the driver's condition. The body was slumped forward with blood on its face, firefighter Dennis Walsh said, noting that the officer "had to reach in the window right past the body. He put the ticket on the inside of the dash and drove off, and here this guy has been dead in the driver's seat for ten or twelve hours."

....

MISSOURI STATE POLICE INVESTIGATING reports of a man changing out of women's clothes outside the Hatton fireworks stand located the suspect. He explained that he was on his way home and wanted to go into the store but didn't know if it was okay to enter dressed in women's clothes.

....

KENNETH PEART, 77, OF IDAHO FALLS, Idaho, reported that he was cheated out of $12,700 by two Buffalo telemarketing companies. A third firm, Capital Punishers Inc., of the Buffalo suburb of North Tonawanda, called and offered to come to his rescue. "They told me that if I sent them $600, they'd get back all the money I lost," Peart told the *Buffalo News*. "They said they knew some bad things happened to me with those other guys, and they were going to help me out." Instead, he said, they helped him out of $600.

WHEN VALUJET AIRLINES, BASED IN AT-
lanta, offered a contest to choose a new market for
the airline to service within a 400-mile radius of that
city, suggestions included San Diego (1,887 miles dis-
tant), San Francisco (2,135 miles away), Nassau (732
miles out), Bermuda and Jamaica. Other choices, such
as Blairsville or Fitzgerald, Georgia, have no commercial airports. Another failed suggestion was Macon,
only a 45-minute drive from Atlanta.

JORDON LAZELLE, 18, OF HAYLING IS-
land, England, had to be hospitalized after he was
stung on the tongue by his pet scorpion when he tried
to give it its usual good-night kiss. Lazelle said that
when he kissed "Twiggy" it grabbed his lip. Then when
he opened his mouth in shock, "he jumped in and
stung me on the tongue—it had never done that
before."

TWO EMPLOYEES OF DELTA AIRLINES, A
mechanic and a customer service agent, were arrested
and fired after they took an empty Boeing 737 on a
mile-long joyride at the Tucson airport.

A TORONTO LAWYER PLUNGED TO HIS death from the 24th floor of a skyscraper when he rammed a window pane with his shoulder while demonstrating the strength of the glass to a group of visiting law students. Police said that he often rammed the windows to prove to colleagues that the windows were unbreakable.

IN GRANTS PASS, OREGON, ANTHONY Roberts, 25, was shot through the eye and skull with an arrow by a friend trying to knock a gas can off his head. The arrow's tip went 8 to 10 inches into Roberts's brain, but caused no brain damage. He lost an eye but was otherwise unhurt. Roberts explained that the friend was shooting the can off his head as an initiation for a rafting and outdoor group called Mountain Men Anonymous, admitting, "I feel really stupid."

WHEN BOULDER, COLORADO, POLICE AR-rested Peter J. Smith, 21, for shooting his 21-year-old roommate in the shoulder, the victim confirmed Smith's story that they were practicing drawing their guns and pointing them at each other, as they did "every once in a while."

STEPHEN STILL, 36, A TOWN ALDERMAN
in Gentry, Arkansas, was charged with murder after
shooting a 22-year-old man in the head while trying to
shoot cans and bottles off his head. Still was using a
.22-caliber rifle with a scope to shoot at the targets
only 15 to 20 feet away. Police said that he had performed the same target practice before.

Dumb with Attitude

BEFORE HIS DEATH IN 1994 AT AGE 81, Yahiya Avraham served 32 years in an Israeli prison for refusing to divorce his wife. Ora Avraham, who married Yahiya when she was 12 and he was 28, applied for divorce in 1950 after 12 years of marriage, explaining that he berated and abused her for not bearing sons. Jewish law says that both parties must agree to a divorce, but Yahiya refused to say the three words needed to make the action final: "I am willing."

He was imprisoned in 1962 as a last resort effort to persuade him and remained there for the rest of his life, consistently refusing pleas to accede. In February 1993, he rejected entreaties from a delegation of seven rabbis, who spent two hours trying to persuade him by promising him freedom, a fancy apartment and religious blessings. One of the rabbis even sang melancholy songs to try to soften the man's heart, but all he said was, "Can't do it, can't do it, go away."

A SOUTH KOREAN MAN PUNCHED HIS brother to death during a fight over North Korea's decision to bar inspectors from its nuclear sites. Police explained that when Kim Il-bong, 27, said he would not care if a war broke out between the two Koreas over the issue, his brother, Kim Il-nam, 29, became angry, accused his brother of being unpatriotic and punched him repeatedly in the face.

JOHN MATTINGLY JR., 26, SERVED HIS 85-year-old grandmother with an eviction notice, claiming that she hadn't paid rent on the duplex they share.

A BUSLOAD OF RUSSIAN SHOPPERS heading for Poland refused to interrupt their trip when one of them died from a heart attack. Instead of turning back to bury the corpse, they left it on the backseat of the bus and continued into Poland. They returned home after several days of bargain hunting.

WHILE DEFENDING A MAN IN D.C. SUPE-rior Court accused of beating his girlfriend's 12-year-old daughter, a Washington attorney announced after three days that he was withdrawing from the case. He explained that he had expected the trial to proceed in a more timely manner and had purchased nonrefundable airline tickets for a vacation. "It's manifestly necessary in my view that you continue the defense of your client," the judge told the attorney. When this plea failed, the judge threatened to hold him in custody to assure his presence in the courtroom. The attorney warned that such a move would only harm his client. "I mean, I'll just be extremely hostile to (the defendant). I'm just going to be totally hostile, totally hostile," he told the judge, who was forced to declare a mistrial.

POLICE IN ELIZABETH, NEW JERSEY, charged Bolaji O. Adeigbola, 24, with firing six shots from a .357 Magnum inside a train station. He had just missed a train to New York and was told he would have to wait an hour for the next one.

KEVIN FRITZE, 24, OF WEST ORANGE,

New Jersey, pleaded guilty to boarding an NJ Transit bus, sitting down behind the driver, brandishing a pistol and ordering the driver not to pick up any more passengers or make any more stops. Fritze, an Essex County courthouse worker, explained that he hijacked the bus because he did not want to be late for work.

IN UTAH, MATTHEW GARDNER ADMITTED

lying when he said he set several fires at the Olympus Care Center. He explained that he figured his confession would send him to prison instead of the Utah State Hospital, where he claimed a Mormon conspiracy denied him coffee. Police speculated that Gardner set the fires in revenge because the center served him decaffeinated coffee during a 1985 interview and then denied him residency. "He has a strong dislike to being served decaffeinated coffee," therapist James Ricciardi told 3rd District Court Judge Anne Stirba. She ordered Gardner to undergo outpatient treatment at a residential facility after telling him that if he didn't comply he would be sent to the Utah State Hospital. Gardner, who has a history of mental illness, vowed to cooperate, explaining that he wanted to recover so he could run for the Utah legislature or for mayor of Salt Lake City.

A SINGER IN A TORONTO KARAOKE CLUB
shot two men in the audience, killing one and seriously
wounding the other, who laughed at his singing. "I
know it sounds hard to believe," said Det. Sgt. Mike
Hamel, "but that appears to be the motive."

A STUDENT AT PENN STATE UNIVERSITY
charged a fellow student with breach of contract after
he failed a test that she hired him to take for her. "It
was an oddball business arrangement," said Cpl. Dana
Leonard. The woman reported the incident to try to
get back a $1,200 stereo she said she paid the student
for taking the exam. University officials said that the
students faced expulsion and up to a year in prison
and a $2,500 fine for violating a state law against sell-
ing academic work.

OSCAR DOMINGUEZ, 45, A SÃO PAULO
psychiatrist, admitted shooting a woman patient to
death while she told him about her sex life. He told
the court, "I couldn't take those nut cases anymore."

WILLIAM M. HOLYFIELD, 35, CHECKED
into the downtown Hilton Hotel in Portland, Oregon,
and paid cash for one night's lodging. He tried to pay
for a second night's stay, but was told the hotel was
booked up because of a convention and that his credit
card was no good. According to police spokesperson
Henry Groepper, Holyfield refused to give up his room,
announcing that he planned to stay there "until the
year 2049." When security guards tried to remove him,
he climbed out his window using knotted bed sheets
as a rope to lower himself to the ground. Instead he
fell three floors, suffering a head injury and multiple
broken bones.

POLICE IN QUESNEL, BRITISH COLUMBIA,
arrested Leon Roger Hetu, 50, after he used a bulldozer
to tear down the house of his girlfriend, Mildred
Stychyshyn. She explained that Hetu, an unemployed
bulldozer operator, became angry when she wouldn't
let him in because he was drunk. Two months earlier,
Hetu had attacked her house with a bulldozer, taking
off the corner where her master bedroom had been.

IN LONG ISLAND, NEW YORK, MARION

Frankson, 41, was accused of having sex with her daughter's 16-year-old boyfriend in the backseat of a car while her husband, William, 42, videotaped them from the front seat. The Franksons propositioned the boy, apparently without the daughter's knowledge, when she brought him home to meet her parents, police said, adding that the boy wore a mask during the taping so he would not be recognized.

AFTER FOUR TRIES, DONEVA CARTER FI-

nally won the Miss Black Colorado beauty pageant in 1993. She resigned less than a month later after reports that she had been sentenced to 90 days in jail and four years probation for forgery. Miss Black Colorado Metroplex pageant officials were considering reinstating her, but when they further learned that she was secretly married, they hastily crowned a new queen. "We could overcome that she had problems in the past with the law and that she had paid the debt to society," said the Reverend Acen Phillips of the pageant advisory committee. "When it came out that she was married, that's one thing we couldn't overcome."

A DENVER MAN AND HIS 12-YEAR-OLD daughter went from classroom to classroom at Martin Luther King Jr. Middle School in search of another student. When they found her, the father instructed his daughter to beat her up. According to police and witnesses, teachers who tried to break up the fight were held back by the father, who kept telling his daughter to "go get that girl and kick her ass."

NIKKI FREY WAS OUSTED AS EDITOR OF A Los Angeles Mensa chapter newsletter for publishing articles in the high-IQ group's publication proposing that people "who are so mentally defective that they cannot live in society should, as soon as they are identified as defective, be humanely dispatched." An article called for similar treatment for the homeless and infirm old people. "I didn't think it was harmful," Frey said of her decision to publish the articles. "I don't think it's even that offensive. Nobody wants to have a deformed child."

HIDEMITSU GOTO OF KAGOSHIMA, JA-pan, forced his daughter to spend four years running the length and breadth of Japan. Starting when she was

6, Fuyo Goto ran 12 to 25 miles a day, covering 15,500 miles. Her father accompanied her on his motorcycle while her younger sister Muna rode in the sidecar. He lectured Fuyo on politics, economics and philosophy as she ran alongside. Admitting that his own dream to run around Japan had been thwarted when he lost a toe and damaged an Achilles tendon in an accident, Goto explained, "I decided to realize my ambition through my daughter. I wanted to see the extent of human ability."

MELVIN DEBALL WAS RIDING A GREY-hound bus from Louisiana to California with his wife and grandson when he began pestering the driver to stop for a smoke break. After the driver told him to sit down, witnesses said Deball opened a window and dived through it head first. Police in Casa Grande, Arizona, said hitting the highway killed him.

DR. STUART M. BERGER, AN AUTHOR OF best-selling diet and health books who contended that his weight-loss programs would result in increased longevity, died on February 23, 1994. At the time, he was 40 years old and weighed 365 pounds.

JAMES KIRBY, 45, ARRESTED FOR SHOOT-
ing a woman in the back as she watched *Schindler's
List* in a San Diego, California, movie theater, told police that he "was so involved with the movie that he
wanted to come to the defense of Jewish people. So
he pulled the gun out and squeezed the trigger." Kirby,
who had recently converted to Judaism, said that he
pulled the trigger but didn't expect the gun to fire.

PATRICK DOYLE, 23, A WITNESS IN A MUR-
der trial in Fonda, New York, appeared in court wearing a T-shirt that read, "If shit could fly, this place
would be an airport." Doyle claimed that it was his
only clean shirt, but the unsympathetic judge sentenced him to 30 days.

A 45-YEAR-OLD MAN IN MERIDEN, CON-
necticut, was accused of dialing 911 at least 25 times
in one day to report a toothache. After several calls in
which he cursed and threatened the 911 dispatchers,
police came to his house and he was charged with
criminal mischief. At the police station, after bail was
set at $6,000, police allowed the man to use the tele-

phone to call a bail bondsman. Instead he proceeded to dial 911 and again curse at the dispatchers.

AFTER WAITING ABOUT 40 MINUTES FOR the owner of a parked pickup truck to return and move the vehicle from in front of his sports car in a San Jose, California, parking garage, Daniel Jensen took a tow hitch from the back of the truck, smashed a window and pushed it out of the way. Questioned by police later, Jensen explained that he was a lawyer and that at his rate of $175 to $200 an hour, his time was too valuable to spend waiting for a tow truck to arrive.

WORKERS AT OREGON'S COQUILLE PUBLIC Library reported that someone used white correction fluid to paint over passages in about a dozen of the library's 25,000 volumes. "They've marked everything from love-swept romances to bestsellers," librarian Molly DePlois said, explaining that most of the deleted passages are sexually explicit. "I'm assuming that it's a single person, someone who has a lot of attention to detail and a lot of time on their hands."

STEVEN ENGELMAN, 38, EXPLAINED TO AN

Ohio court that he shot at a passing car because the car's license plate reminded him of an incident eight years earlier in which he was stabbed in a bar. The plate read JABU which Engelman took to mean "jab you."

THE ISRAELI ARMY ANNOUNCED IT WOULD

court-martial Cpt. Shai Engler in response to complaints from parents of men newly transferred to his unit that he repeatedly bit the men on the buttocks after having subordinates bring them into his tent and pull down their pants. Engler explained he bit new troops to motivate them and "to test the sergeants' cheek muscles."

IN FLORIDA, JEREMIAH JOHNSON, 18, AR-

rived at court to answer a charge of driving without a license, but a bailiff told him he couldn't enter the courtroom wearing shorts. Johnson left briefly, then returned wearing nothing. Polk County Judge Michael Raiden sentenced him to 179 days in jail for contempt of court.

Bunk! Don't You Believe It!

IN TEXAS, MORE THAN 500 PEOPLE mobbed the Fort Worth Central Library and started throwing books from the shelves. They were looking for $5 and $10 bills supposedly placed in the books by Dallas radio station KYNG-FM. It urged listeners to go on a treasure hunt for the bills, which it said had been placed as bookmarks in the fiction section.

The mob told stunned librarians that they were in search of $10,000. One librarian described crowds of people running down stairways screaming, "Where's fiction? Where's fiction?" Many started climbing bookshelves and over each other. When it was all over, at least 3,500 books wound up on the floor, many with cracked spines, and ripped pages and covers. At least 100 books were beyond repair.

After the trashing, the station admitted just $100 had been put in books and that it had expected fewer than 30 people to show up to look for the cash. The program director explained that the promotion was designed to "get people to think about when was the last time they went to the library."

DEEJAY DAVE RICKARDS OF KGB-FM IN San Diego broadcasted a report on April Fools' Day 1993 that a space shuttle would be landing at the city's Montgomery Field at 8:30 A.M. Despite the fact that no shuttle was then in orbit and that it would be physically impossible to land the shuttle at the small airport, hundreds of families descended on the scene, video camcorders in hand. The result was a massive traffic jam and hundreds of people late to school and work. Richards said that he was "looking for a good scambo for April Fools' Day. I just light these bombs, and then I run away."

ON SUNDAY NIGHT, OCTOBER 30, 1994, CBS broadcast the made-for-TV movie *Without Warning*. Presented in the format of a live, breaking news story, the tale of asteroids impacting on Earth resulted in hundreds of telephone calls to CBS affiliates from viewers around the country, despite the presence of disclaimers at every commercial break explaining that "None of what you are seeing is actually happening." Interviewed the next day, veteran broadcast journalist Sander Vanocur, who played the news anchor in the movie, asked, "Has America lost its capacity to read?"

Lost and
Then Some

KERI LENOX, 20, LEFT HER HOME IN BEL-
videre, Illinois, to look for work in nearby Rockford.
She got lost, however, and ended up in South Bend,
Indiana. After writing her parents that she had reached
Rockford safely, she got lost again and turned up in
Philadelphia, then Houlton, Maine, where a U.S. Border Patrol agent found her three weeks later. "I think
she didn't plan on getting lost," said Boone County
Det. Perry Gay, "but when she did, she wanted everyone to think she knew what she was doing and then
she would get herself out of it."

POLICE IN KIRKENES, A NORTHERN NOR-
wegian town bordering Russia, found a 72-year-old
Swedish man who had been driving for three days
without stopping—in the wrong direction. According
to officer Bjorn Syversen, the man and his 16-year-old
grandson were returning from a fishing trip some 65
miles from their home in central Sweden. The man
turned north instead of south and, even after stopping
several times to ask directions when he crossed into
Norway, he continued north beyond the Arctic Circle.
The journey ended only after the exhausted man fell
asleep and crashed into a ditch. "They misread the
map," Syversen said. "After three days the old man
simply couldn't drive anymore."

A DETROIT CITY BUS DRIVER GOT LOST
trying to find the bus depot and instead drove 200
miles north for four hours before state police stopped
him and turned him around.

Dumb Luck

IN LOS ANGELES, PATRICE HASLIP, 34, reportedly shot and wounded her husband, John, for incorrectly filling out a mail sweepstakes entry form, then tossing it in the trash. Det. Joe Martinez said she explained that she fired a .22-caliber bullet at John Haslip, 36, through the bathroom door after she became incensed because her husband had "jeopardized her chance to be on national TV."

GERMAN TOURIST CHRISTA LANDWEHR, 58, arranged for a vacation to Costa Rica, but her travel agent booked her on the wrong flight and she arrived 4,900 miles off course in San Jose. At the airport, Landwehr, who speaks no English, hailed a cab and asked for the Ritz-Carlton Hotel, but the driver assumed she meant the Fairmont Hotel. She tried to check into the hotel by using Costa Rican money, but after communicating with the night manager using gestures, she paid with traveler's checks instead. She learned of her mistake the next morning when she had breakfast with a German-speaking hotel employee. By 10:30 she was on a plane to Costa Rica.

GERMAN TOURIST JOHANN GRZEGANEK,

24, spent 10 months in jail in Fort Lauderdale, Florida, because his urgent need to go to the bathroom was mistaken for a bomb threat. The problem started aboard a flight to Germany when Grzeganek got up to use the rest room while the seat belt sign was on. He explained his bladder was "going to explode," but a flight attendant told him to sit down. When he protested, "No, no, no, the roof would go," the attendant thought Grzeganek was referring to a bomb. He was taken into custody when the plane turned around and landed.

IN FRANCE, A PASSENGER TRAVELING

aboard a high-speed train from Paris to Toulouse dropped his wallet down a chemical toilet, reached in to scoop it out and wound up with his hand stuck in the bowl. He hit the emergency alarm, and the train stopped. Unable to free his hand, rescue workers spent two hours cutting the toilet out of the floor, then sent the man to the hospital with the toilet bowl wrapped around his arm.

A U.S. ARMY GULF WAR VETERAN ENtitled to a check from the government for $183.69, instead received $836,939.19 due to a computer error. Charged with spending the money and filing a false tax return, the man argued that it was a gift from God, as it came to him after an incident in which he paused on a lonely road at night and prayed to God for the means to be self-sufficient.

BARRY LYN STOLLER, 38, OF KENT, Washington, wrote the makers of Ex-Lax, claiming the product didn't work and demanding reimbursement of the $1.99 he paid. The New Jersey–based Sandoz Corporation immediately issued a refund but mistook the amount, using Stoller's zip code. After the error was discovered, King County authorities found Stoller had deposited the check for $98,002, withdrawn the money eight days later, closed his account and left the area without a trace.

POLICE IN BARCELONA, SPAIN, SAID THAT
a man who won $374,000 in a lottery got into an argument with his family over how to share the money and wound up stabbing his 17-year-old sister to death. When police arrived on the scene, the man jumped from the family's second-floor apartment to escape. After he landed in the street below, he was hit by a car and hospitalized in intensive care.

IN FOGGIA, ITALY, ARMANDO PINELLI, 70,
argued with another man over who should sit in the only chair in the shade of a palm tree. Pinelli won. When he sat down, the tree fell over on him and killed him.

IN BRAZIL, MARÍA BENOIZA NASCIMENTO,
39, an unemployed mother of seven who lives in a one-room shack, burned her winning $60,000 lottery ticket.

She explained that her Assembly of God minister told her she would go to hell if she took the devil's money.

AFTER AN AUSTRALIAN BANK ISSUED A check for $1.5 million instead of $1,550 and deposited it in the account of a Melbourne couple, they went on a week-long spending spree that cleaned out the account. When police asked the wife, Terry Prudzinski, why she did not question the deposit, the 42-year-old accountant explained, "I had an expectation of an inheritance." Skeptical Magistrate Jack Tobin ordered her to stand trial for theft.

IN STOCKTON, CALIFORNIA, MOHAMMAD Idrees Kussair, 43, was cleared of criminal charges after a bank accidentally coded a check for $100,000 as one for $1 million and credited his account. After using the money to pay off rental properties and to take a trip to Pakistan, Kussair explained that he assumed a relative in Pakistan had wired the money to his account.

AFTER A METEORITE CRASHED ONTO A
village roadside in Thailand's Petchabun province, local residents erected an altar nearby and began to
gather at the site to pray for good luck. Many began
to purchase lottery tickets, using numbers that they
said they could see on the meteorite. The governor of
the province then ordered the 37-pound meteorite
seized, claiming that objects falling from the sky are
the property of the government. Armed police guards
had to be assigned to protect it after villagers began
marching in protest to have the rock returned.

IN AUSTRALIA, A $1-A-CHANCE RAFFLE
aimed at raising money to help Queensland surfer
Trudy Todd, 18, continue competing on the world professional surfing circuit offered as first prize a fling
with a prostitute. Todd's parents approved the fund-
raiser when a prostitute offered her services after
Todd's father rescued her from a male attacker.

WARREN E. SMITH FILED A $3 MILLION
lawsuit against Roanoke, Virginia, palm reader Lola
Rose Miller, charging that she sold him losing lottery
numbers. He said she persuaded him to give her

$75,724, which was almost all of his money, including his retirement fund, for the numbers to win a $3 million lottery jackpot. Smith said Miller, also known as Miss Stella, told him that he didn't win because someone in his family had placed a curse on him.

HUNDREDS OF READERS OF SOUTH AFrica's *Star* newspaper lined up outside its offices in Johannesburg to collect their $270 prize for having the winning number in a contest. Editor Peter Sullivan told them the winning number was a typographical error and that the paper was not obligated to pay out any winnings. Sullivan had to be driven off in a police car when enraged entrants refused to accept the explanation and demanded money. The paper paid out $97,000 in consolation prizes of up to $27.

GLEN WOODCOCK, 31, DROVE HIS FORD Bronco onto an army bombing range, then got stuck just as soldiers prepared to open fire. Military police at Fort Bragg, North Carolina, arrested the still-unsuspecting Woodcock after he walked across the range, which is littered with thousands of pounds of unexploded ammunition and pockmarked with bomb craters, and asked some soldiers to help him move his truck. "Why or how he did not step on something and

blow himself totally up is a miracle," garrison commander Col. Woodrow Wilson said. Since retrieving
the vehicle would be too dangerous, it was left as a
target.

WHEN HONG KONG POLICE RAIDED THE

home of attempted robbery suspect Chung Hung-fat,
22, they discovered a live, 66-mm antitank rocket,
packed with high explosives, sitting on top of his television set. He told them he found it seven years earlier
while walking near an army firing range and kept it as
a knickknack. Police said the rocket could have been
set off with a bump, such as changing stations, and
would have demolished Chung's apartment.

FLORIDA BUSINESS EXECUTIVE RICHARD T.

Clary, 41, was accused of embezzling about $500,000
from his employer to support a $5,000-a-week lottery
habit. Assistant State's Attorney Timothy Collins said
that in three years of playing the lottery with other
people's money, Clary apparently won only about
$2,500, which he simply used to buy more losing
tickets.

2.

WHO'S IN CHARGE HERE?

Hail, Hail Freedonia! (And Other Government Intelligence)

IN 1990, THE CUSTOMS SERVICE launched six helium-filled balloons equipped with surveillance equipment to detect drug smuggling along the Mexican border. The balloons cost $90 million to build and $30 million to operate during the 30 months in which agents seized only 3,000 pounds of marijuana and nine weapons. Even though this works out to $40,000 for each pound of marijuana seized, Sen. Dennis DeConcini, D-Arizona, defended the program by pointing out that the low numbers prove the balloons are deterring smuggling activity.

THE LOS ANGELES CENTRAL LIBRARY, refurbished after two 1986 incidents of arson, reopened with an uncertified fire suppression system. Officials said that until certification was complete, eight city workers would patrol the building around the clock looking for blazes.

AFTER THE U.S. ARMY JOURNAL *MILITARY Review* printed an article by Charles T. Harrison entitled "Hell in a Hand Basket: The Threat of Portable Nuclear Weapons," it learned that the author—identified as a commercial pilot, a member of the Mensa Society and "a freelance researcher for the Pentagon and the U.S. Department of Energy"—also was a resident of the Middle Tennessee Mental Health Institute. He had been committed nine years earlier as a paranoid schizophrenic after killing his mother. Harrison, 47, was also responsible for writing numerous letters over the years to the FBI and the Secret Service claiming responsibility for a number of assassination plots against world leaders, including the pope.

Military Review is published at the Army's Command and General Staff College in Fort Levenworth, Kansas. Its circulation includes 19,000 senior officers and foreign subscribers. Informed of the situation, editor-in-chief Col. John Reitz explained that editors who spoke to Harrison by phone did not know what kind of hospital it was and assumed that Harrison was elderly and sick.

Harrison challenged the diagnosis of paranoid schizophrenia, explaining that he killed his mother in an argument over his insistence that the Bible counseled the murder of one's parents. Harrison said that when his mother came at him with a gun, "I got my pistol. I shot her first."

THE BRYN MELYN THERAPY CENTER IN Wales lost funding for a $2,247-a-week program that sent young hoodlums on vacation as a "character-building" exercise. Politicians expressed outrage when one young offender was arrested on a drunk-driving charge after returning from an 80-day African safari with his social worker, prompting Home Secretary Michael Howard to declare, "I can only think those responsible for this decision had access to more money than sense."

THE FORT WORTH, TEXAS, CITY COUNCIL authorized a program using federal grants to pay local gang members $5 an hour to work as antiviolence counselors.

TWO WEEKS AFTER AUTHORITIES IN MA-
honing County, Ohio, charged Eric Jones, 47, with killing his wife, they dropped the charges. Youngstown
police Lieut. David Williams explained that Jones was
set free because he may need a heart transplant and
authorities didn't want to be responsible for the bill,
which could top $250,000.

POLICE IN PRINCE GEORGE'S COUNTY,
Maryland, began visiting predominantly black high
schools to teach students the proper way to behave
when being arrested.

THE CZECH REPUBLIC BEGAN PROSECUT-
ing Prague restaurants for "crimes against cuisine."
The European reported that since shedding the Com-
munist yoke, when the state prosecuted deviation from
official recipes in the government-authorized cook-
book, the Czechs have experienced a spate of raids by
Prague taste police assuring traditional standards for
reintroduced ethnic dishes and charging cooks with,
among other things, "dumpling subversion."

AUTHORITIES INVESTIGATING A FIRE IN IS-
lamabad, Pakistan, that gutted the six-story white mar-
ble parliament building, reported that it was sparked
by wiring that overheated after 300 lights had been left
on for six years. The fire wasn't discovered for several
hours because the fire alarm had been shut off. When
firefighters finally located the fire, they couldn't get to
it because the doors were locked and guards with keys
could not be found, making it necessary to break down
the doors. By this time, the fire was out of control.

THE MOUNT LYELL MINING AND RAILWAY
Company of Queenstown, Tasmania, tried to clean up
an area devastated by acid rain caused by its copper
smelter until the Tasmanian government ordered the
company to stop revegetating the mountains and fer-
tilizing the seedlings it planted. The bare hills are the
town's major tourist attraction, according to local
member of parliament Peter Schulze, who noted, "Artists come from all over to paint them."

THE   ENVIRONMENTAL   PROTECTION
Agency ordered the city of San Diego, California, to
stop its cleanup of a portion of the Tijuana River. The

EPA explained that the cleanup would cause irreparable harm to the "sewage-based ecology."

....

BOLIVIA, A LANDLOCKED COUNTRY, HAS
72 naval installations and a 6,000-member navy, whose main job is to patrol the world's largest lake, the 110-mile-long Lake Titicaca. But a naval cadet's 12 months of duty are mostly consumed with organizing regattas, first-aid instruction and cleaning trash from rivers. A 240-mile-long strip of Pacific coast did belong to Bolivia until Chile annexed it in 1879. The naval command is not content with simply patrolling lakes and rivers. "Without a coastline, Bolivia is like a man without eyes or arms. We are suffocated and incomplete," said Admiral Miguel Alvarez Delgado. Each March the country celebrates the "Day of the Sea," and the annual Miss Bolivia beauty contest always includes a Miss Coastline.

....

THE IDAHO DEPARTMENT OF MOTOR VE-
hicles denied a handicapped license plate to Jay Dula, even though he applied in person, because he didn't have a doctor's note verifying his condition. Dula has one leg, having lost all but six inches of the other to cancer at age 13. He does not wear an artificial leg and showed the DMV clerk his handicapped plates from

California, from where he moved. Rules are rules, said Transportation Department special plates supervisor Candy Smith, explaining, "Even if he had an artificial limb and he took it off and slapped it on the counter, we'd still need a physician's statement stating what the disability is and whether it's permanent or temporary."

Dula settled for a vanity license plate: GYMP.

A U.S. AIRDROP TO FEED RWANDANS missed the target by a half-mile, scattering 10 tons of food bundles over terrified Rwandan refugees, who thought they were being bombed. The Associated Press reported that one bundle narrowly missed a UN helicopter and another almost hit a school. Others fell deep among banana trees, and workers said they expected to salvage only about half of it. Although the three C-130s did deliver another 10 tons on target, prompting the U.S. Army's European Command to declare the mission a success, Alison Campbell of CARE decried it as a publicity stunt. Noting that a 540-ton convoy of food was arriving from Uganda, she said, "The twenty tons are irrelevant."

A JUMBO-SIZED POISONOUS PLANT BRED in the Soviet Union and brought to Poland in the 1970s is spreading like wildfire across that country. Dubbed

"Stalin's revenge," the plant towers up to 13 feet tall with leaves the size of open umbrellas. Authorities reported that growing numbers of people are coming to hospitals with skin burns caused by touching the plant, some severe enough to leave scars. The plant was devised by biologists during Stalin's reign to use as cattle feed. Cows who were fed the plant did produce richer milk, but it also turned out to be bitter.

TO MAKE SURE ITS SOLDIERS PASS A promotion exam, the Belgian army gives candidates both the questions and answers in advance. The exam, covering arms, tactics and chemical warfare, has 85 multiple-choice questions. Candidates must correctly answer 20.

A WEEK AFTER THE BRITISH GOVERNMENT said it would allow some police officers to carry their weapons instead of keeping them locked in the trunk of their squad cars, two loaded police revolvers fell off the roof of a squad car and landed in the road in Blackburn. A passerby found them and turned them in. The revolvers reportedly were left on the roof during a shift change.

CONNECTICUT'S ESCAPE RATE OF FIVE IN-
mates a month from its 22 prisons prompted concern
among residents of Cheshire, which has four prisons.
State and local authorities responded by announcing
they were buying 300 telephone pagers to give to
homeowners living near the prisons so they could be
notified immediately of jail breaks and disturbances.
Kathy Needham, chairperson of the Cheshire Prison
Advisory Committee, praised the pagers, but pointed
out that inmates "might have been out a few hours
before anyone knows they're missing."

NOTING THAT $2.8 BILLION SPENT ON A
defense system against enemy missiles created useful
commercial applications from military research find-
ings, a Ballistic Missile Defense Organization report
said that one result of this technology transfer was
"pizza delivery operations to keep pizza hot and crisp
for two hours."

THE AGRICULTURE DEPARTMENT, INTER-
preting the Animal Welfare Act, decreed that rats, mice
and birds are not animals. As such, they are exempt
from strict rules governing treatment of laboratory

creatures. The Humane Society of the United States and the Animal Legal Defense Fund objected to their exclusion and sued. They won, but the department appealed.

The U.S. Court of Appeals decided in favor of the Agriculture Department on a technicality: Only those directly injured by the Animal Welfare Act can sue to change it. Martin Stephens, HSUS vice president, said further appeals would be hard "unless we can teach these animals to represent themselves."

AFTER NINE POLICE OFFICERS ON A NARcotics raid at an apartment building in Coventry, England, squeezed into an elevator made for eight, it stalled. The officers wound up being trapped for 45 minutes until resident Eddie Laidle heard their cries for help. "I told them I would get the police," he said, "and they shouted, 'We *are* the bloody police—get the fire brigade!'"

TOO MANY TRUCK DRIVERS FALL ASLEEP at the wheel, the National Transportation Safety Board concluded in 1994 after poring over a year's reports of fatal accidents involving trucks, because they're sleepy.

AFTER A LENGTHY, OFTEN HEATED DE-
bate, diplomats at a summit of the 53-nation Conference on Security and Cooperation in Europe agreed
"in principle" to change the group's name to the Organization for Security and Cooperation in Europe.

IN CHINA, 404 PEOPLE DIED AND 1,028
were injured in traffic accidents during the first year's
operation of a 164-mile expressway linking Beijing and
Shijiazhuang. Authorities blamed the high fatality rate
on a middle lane that allows cars on both sides of the
road to pass, making head-on collisions almost inevi-
table if two drivers going in opposite directions decide
to pass at the same time.

WASHINGTON, D.C., BUSINESSES THAT
mailed their quarterly corporate tax payments due September 30, 1994, using the city's preaddressed mailing
label had their envelopes returned stamped "Box
Closed for Nonpayment of Rent." District officials explained that two post office boxes, including the one
used to collect corporate taxes, had been closed since
that June because the city neglected to pay the $405

annual fee, although they claimed that postal officials never sent a reminder that the box rents were due.

....

WHEN OFFICIALS IN WELLINGTON, NEW Zealand, applied for a building permit for a new police station, they discovered that the city's new building code required that all prisoners must have immediate access to an exit in case of fire. "It means that if you have to put prisoners behind lock and key," Regional Commander Murray Jackson said, "you have to give them a key so they can get out."

....

JAPAN'S NUCLEAR AGENCY PRODUCED A promotional videotape to allay public fears about its plan to import 30 tons of plutonium as fuel for power plants, claiming, among other things, that the highly radioactive substance is safe enough to drink. The Power Reactor and Nuclear Fuel Development Corporation's video, which is aimed at school-age children, features an animated character named Mr. Pluto, who contends that plutonium's dangers have been exaggerated. In one scene, Mr. Pluto shakes the hand of a youngster who is drinking a mug of plutonium-laced soda while the narration says that if plutonium were ingested, most of it would pass through the body without harm.

Critics of the agency noted that plutonium is actually toxic to humans because it is absorbed by bone marrow. Inhaling .0001 of a gram can induce lung cancer.

A BRITISH PRISON HAD TO SPEND $128,000 on new locks after inmates saw a close-up photograph of the warden unlocking a cell and copied the keys.

ABOUT 100 SPANISH OLIVE GROWERS complained that they had not received their annual European Community subsidies, even though they had filed the required paperwork. Authorities at the regional office in Andalucia found that their computer was not programmed to recognize the letter n with a tilde. All the farmers who failed to receive their checks had names with tildes.

IN KOREA, THE SEOUL METROPOLITAN Police Administration responded to complaints that the police emergency number was sometimes busy by installing two fax machines for people who can't get through on the phone to report crimes.

CUBA'S HEALTH MINISTRY WARNED PEOple not to use glass tubes from television sets to prepare home-made alcoholic beverages. Tight rationing of commercially produced beverages, including rum, triggered a wave of home brewing, often using discarded TV tubes, according to the ministry, which announced a crackdown. "This is an extremely dangerous practice," it explained, "which could have serious health consequences because of the toxic substances with which the tubes are impregnated."

IN ACCORDANCE WITH A 1986 CALIFORNIA environmental regulation, Pacific Gas and Electric mailed its customers a warning about the potential dangers of sand. The notice pointed out that sandblasting at the power company's plants "can release sand, . . . [which] naturally contains crystalline silica, a chemical known to the State of California to cause cancer."

NEW YORK STATE PROPOSED MAKING
prison inmates pay state and local sales taxes on purchases at prison commissaries, explaining that doing
so could raise $520,000 a year. State prison officials
pointed out it would cost $1.5 million to hire a clerk
at each of the 68 prisons to make sure nobody cheats.

MICHAEL BALAGUS, DIRECTOR OF COM-
munications for the leader of Canada's New Democratic Party, resigned after it was disclosed that he
used a U.S. company to produce a video criticizing the
Canadian government for exporting jobs to the United
States. Balagus explained that he hired a Washington,
D.C., firm to make the $35,000, six-minute video be-
cause he believed that no Canadian company could do
the job on short notice.

KUWAIT'S CHARITY COMMITTEE FOR THE
Marriage Project urged married men to take more
wives (up to the Islamic legal limit of four) in order to
deal with the problem of "spinsterhood." Saying there
were too many unmarried Kuwaiti women, the charity
offered men up to $2,800 in loans, cheap kitchenware
and free furniture.

BUDGET CUTS IN CALIFORNIA SLOWED
production at 22 state prisons that turn out furniture,
textiles and clothing for state agencies and public
schools, but even inmates with no work to do still reported to their jobs since every day they work reduces
their sentences by a day. "If there's no work, you either
do nothing or you get sent back to your cell," said
Roger Golden, 31, serving three years for petty theft.
"But you still get a day off your time."

THE DEARBORN, MICHIGAN, POLICE DE-
partment suspended Officer Brian Yinger for three
days and ordered him to undergo psychiatric evalua-
tion because he writes the numeral seven by crossing
the downstroke, the way Europeans do, to distinguish
it from the numeral one. Noting that he had been
crossing his sevens for 30 years, beginning in the seventh grade and including 15 years with the Dearborn
police, Yinger said, "I've never had a problem before."
Explaining that Yinger was suspended because he had
defied an order to stop the practice, Police Chief Deziel
said that Yinger's sevens were confusing clerks who
type reports.

IN PHOENIX, ARIZONA, OFFICIALS CONceded that new bilingual signs put up at Sky Harbor International Airport to help visitors from Mexico were riddled with incorrect words, misspellings, mixed tenses and genders. A sign intended to warn arriving travelers who don't declare plants, fruits, vegetables and meats that they would be fined, instead read *Violadores Seran Finados* (Violators Will Be Deceased). Another, announcing the drinking age, omitted a tilde in the word *ano*, changing its meaning from year to anus. City Manager Frank Fairbanks admitted, "The airport hired a poor translator."

AFTER YEARS OF COMPLAINING ABOUT their neighbors' constantly barking dogs, the Hills family in Kittery, Maine, finally convinced the authorities to take action. Police issued the first summons to the Hills's son, Henry Paradis, for creating a nuisance by barking back at the dogs.

BEFORE BILL CLINTON'S BUS TRIP FROM Charlottesville, Virginia, to Washington, D.C., for his inauguration, the Virginia Department of Transportation assigned a special unit to clean up any roadkill along the President-elect's route.

THE LOS ANGELES DEPARTMENT OF Building and Safety ordered an adult nightclub, the Odd Ball Cabaret, to close its main attraction: a shower enclosure where nude dancers performed for male customers. Officials explained that the enclosure had no wheelchair access, denying people in wheelchairs the opportunity to dance nude, even though none complained they were denied jobs because they couldn't get wheelchairs in the shower. Ron Shigeta, head of the department's Disabled Access Division, explained that the law is the law, no matter how ridiculous it might seem to some people.

THE ARMY ACKNOWLEDGED IN 1994 THAT during the cold war, scientists, curious how easy it would be for enemies to spoil the nation's meat supply, concluded that the best way to find out was for them to sneak up on cows and spray them with deodorant.

IN 1994 THE ACTING SECRETARY OF
State of California, Tony Miller, approved the circulation of petitions for a November ballot initiative that
would mandate that violent criminals, upon their release from prison, submit to having identification numbers "implanted on their faces." The initiative also
makes it clear that to "taunt or harass" a person bearing such identification numbers would be a misde-
meanor offense.

A .3-KILOTON NUCLEAR BOMB WAS DIS-
covered sitting at the bottom of a mine shaft at a test
site in Kazakhstan. The bomb was placed there in 1991
shortly before the Soviet Union collapsed and was simply forgotten in the ensuing chaos.

RIGHT AFTER THE INDIAN GOVERNMENT
ordered dairy farmers to move their cattle out of the
city of Delhi because the animals were producing too
much dung—about 15,000 tons each month—and
overpowering the city's sewer system, the farmers
were outraged to learn that the government was considering importing dung from the Netherlands to promote organic farming. Said Mukhiya Gurjar, president

of the Delhi Dairy Union, "There is no shortfall of dung in our country, and there never will be."

THE ADMINISTRATOR OF MONTANA'S Corrections Division resigned after it was revealed that he rewarded three women prisoners for their good behavior by taking them out to dinner at a Red Lobster restaurant in Billings. One of the three was serving a life sentence for murder. The administrator later noted that he "made a serious judgment error."

IN 1994 THE FEDERAL GOVERNMENT RULED that 90-year-old Altona Brown's coffin, a $2,946 oak box she bought in advance, was not a "burial receptacle" but was a "profitable asset" and denied her $30 a month in Supplemental Security Income and Medicaid benefits unless she first sold the coffin. The government also wanted Brown to sell the beaded moccasins, skin mittens and rugs she had crafted as part of a native American burial ritual. Denied Medicaid, Brown, who is blind, ran up a $60,000 debt at a Fairbanks, Alaska, nursing home where she lives. Only a strong public outcry made the government reverse its decision.

THE DAYTON, OHIO, DAILY NEWS RE-

ported that the Pentagon continued salaries and benefits for 680 military personnel who were behind bars
after being convicted of murder, rape, child molesta-
tion and lesser crimes. The total cost to taxpayers was
more than $1 million a month.

IN ACCORDANCE WITH A SAN FRANCISCO

city ordinance requiring that up to 2 percent of the cost
of new public buildings be spent on art furnishings, a
new $53.5 million 440-bed jail allocated $600,000 to
buy, among other things, a $22,701 60-foot-long, jade
green couch. It is an eight-piece sectional hand-crafted
by an exclusive city furniture store, sits 30 people and
will be used functionally for people in a waiting area.

The jail also features two computerized skylights,
costing $64,000, that track the sun, and meditation atri-
ums costing $70,000. "If you're going to spend fifty mil-
lion dollars," Sheriff Michael Hennessey said, "why not
make it look nice?"

Unfortunately, only half of the jail was scheduled to
open by the end of the year because the project was
so over budget that the city couldn't afford to hire
enough people to staff the whole facility.

FRANCE'S STATE-OWNED ELECTRIC COMpany cut off power at the prime minister's house in 1995 after its records showed Premier Edouard Balladur's $343 payment was late. Electricité de France, blaming "an unjustified procedural error," switched power back on the next day.

THE RUSSIAN POWER COMPANY ARKHEnergo shut off electricity to nuclear submarine plants in the Arctic port city of Severodvinsk in 1994. Regional governor Pavel Balakshin said the city's defense plants had $29 million in unpaid electric bills.

Within 24 hours, Moscow's power authority cut off power to the central command for Russia's nuclear missile forces for failing to pay its overdue electric bill. The power authority said the Strategic Rocket Forces owed $1 million.

UKRAINIAN ENERGY OFFICIALS ANnounced strict rationing measures for the capital of Kiev. Hot water would be supplied to apartments for only three hours a day. Street lights and illuminated billboards would be turned off. When Deputy Prime Minister Anatoly Dyuba also cut television broadcasting to four hours a day, however, so many viewers complained that a week later President Leonid Kuchma overrode Dyuba and ordered full broadcasts resumed.

ANCHORAGE, ALASKA, REQUESTED AN exemption from an Environmental Protection Agency rule requiring cities to remove at least 30 percent of "organic waste" from incoming sewage before treating it. Officials pointed out that the city had so little organic waste to begin with that its sewage before treatment was cleaner than most cities' sewage after treatment. The EPA, nevertheless, insisted that the city comply with the rule, forcing it to have to pay fish processors to dump unused fish parts into city sewer so there would be enough organic waste to remove.

STOCKHOLM'S POLICE COLLEGE HAD TO cancel a lesson on dealing with drunk drivers because half the trainee officers had been out drinking the night before and officials doubted they had sobered up enough to drive. "Three of the lads said that they had drunk six or seven strong beers each," said academy head instructor Krister Nyberg. "We must have limits. You can't be at the police academy while smelling of alcohol."

A 1991 COLORADO BILL SOUGHT TO OUT-
law spreading lies about fruits and vegetables. That
measure was widely ridiculed and vetoed by Gov. Roy
Romer, who said he feared it would infringe on First
Amendment rights to free speech. Since Romer's veto,
at least seven states have enacted similar produce
hate-crime laws. Louisiana's measure is identical to the
Colorado proposal.

THE EL PASO, TEXAS, CITY COUNCIL
voted to spend $112,000 to hire a private security firm
to guard the city's police station.

MUNICIPAL OFFICIALS IN CAP D'AGDE,
site of France's biggest international nudist colony, put
up warning signs: NUDITY OBLIGATORY, and hired special
police to ensure that people using the beach take their
clothes off. Pointing out that extreme sunburn was the
only exception, Mayor Gerard Paillou called the growing invasion of clothed vacationers "intolerable." He
said the action was necessary because more and more
beach users are "simply refusing to get undressed."

THE FEDERAL AVIATION ADMINISTRATION
cited the city of Fort Worth, Texas, for lax security at
Meachem Field. As a shortcut to nearby restaurants,
student pilots were allowed to walk across an active
runway.

IN OCTOBER 1994, THE U.S. GOVERNMENT
announced a $55 million reduction in funding for food
banks and other programs that feed Americans living
below the poverty level. That same day, the government also announced in would spend $47 million to
train Haiti's police force.

AFTER NORTHERN IRELAND'S IRISH RE-
publican Army announced a cease-fire in September
1994, British Prime Minister John Major ended a five-
year-old policy banning the voices of IRA leaders on
British radio or television broadcasts. Because of the
policy, whenever British TV showed news clips of IRA
leaders, it had to hire actors to supply the voices.

BRITAIN'S MINISTRY OF DEFENSE SPENT
$189 million to build and equip a bomb-proof spy bunker beneath its Whitehall headquarters. In case of war, defense chiefs and other key personnel would take refuge there to command forces. When the project was authorized in 1982, officials planned to house 40 to 50 key people. Those not on the list began campaigning to be added, three times causing the bunker to be enlarged. By 1988, nearly 500 people had persuaded officials that they were essential enough to save.

WITHIN MONTHS OF BEING RELEASED
from prison, where he spent four years for molesting 5-year-old and 7-year-old girls, Michael Everett Martin, 47, received a penile implant at a Veterans Affairs hospital. "It wasn't to make me more proficient," Martin explained, "it was to have some degree of normalcy."

SINCE THE END OF THE COLD WAR, PO-
land's elite spy school has fallen on hard times, according to Warsaw's *Gazeta Wyborcza*, whose reporters made an unprecedented visit behind the school's closed doors. No longer able to recruit the best students, "we try to attract the best of the medi-

ocre," said the secret school's unnamed commander. "We can't afford more."

THE SUPREME COURT UPHELD A RULING
that cut off disability benefits to Paul E. Spragens of Wyoming, who has no use of his arms and limited use of his legs, because he earned $349.26 a month as a book indexer by typing with his toes. Federal rules deny benefits to disabled people who earn more than $300 a month.

FROM 1981 THROUGH 1992, SWEDEN
spent $480 million looking for foreign submarines snooping in its waters, believed to be Russians. Sweden committed ships, patrol boats, surveillance planes, helicopters with sonar probes, commandos in rubber rafts or kayaks, divers and guards with night-vision equipment, and frequently detonated depth charges to force the intruders to the surface. No intruder was ever found, and none of the suspicious activity was ever traced to foreign submarines. According to a 1995 Defense Ministry report to the cabinet, the intruders were probably minks. The report pointed out that minks and some other aquatic animals produce the same sound patterns as submarines when detected by hydrophonic instruments.

DUTCH MINISTER OF JUSTICE HIRSCH
Ballin announced that prison inmates would have to
pay to be locked up, explaining that the money was
needed to pay for new cells. Prisoners would be
charged 40 guilders ($21) a day, the price of a cheap
bed and breakfast but a fraction of the actual cost of
keeping an inmate. Inmates receive 50 guilders a day
pocket money and state benefits, enabling some to ac-
cumulate considerable savings during their term. The
government's pay-for-your-stay proposal prompted the
main prisoners' organization, the Union of Lawbreak-
ers, to call for a minimum wage for prisoners to avoid
"a lot of hardship." Union spokesperson Eric van de
Maale said, "People in jail are already paying their debt
to society. If they are forced to pay for bed and board
they will be forced to go out and rob another bank
when their sentence is served."

The Politics
of Dumb

BOSTON NEWSPAPERS AND TELEVISION
stations featured photographs of Massachusetts Port
Authority Executive Director Stephen E. Tocco, wearing a hard hat and protective glasses, using a sledge-
hammer to smash a 25-foot-long cinder block wall to
mark the start of a $1.2 billion modernization of Logan
International Airport. The Port Authority later admitted that the wall was built two days before the ceremony, using donated labor, for $15.93. "We wanted a
very dramatic visual," spokesperson Christina A. Cas-
sotis said, explaining that the wall Port Authority officials wanted to knock down is made of solid
concrete. "You would have had to have a bulldozer to
knock it over, which didn't seem appropriate."

SAN FRANCISCO VOTERS NARROWLY AP-
proved an initiative to give Police Officer Bob Geary,
53, the right to carry his ventriloquist dummy on patrol. Geary said he began using the dummy as a non-
confrontational way of dealing with panhandling,
domestic disputes and other situations unlikely to develop into serious trouble, but his superiors ordered
him to stop. The city's Board of Supervisors approved
a resolution giving Geary the right to carry the puppet,
but Mayor Frank Jordan refused to sign it, prompting
Geary to start petitions to put the issue on the November 1993 ballot. He estimated the drive cost about
$10,000 of his own money, and Registrar of Voters Ger-
maine Wong said it cost the city about $50,000.

FORMER COLORADO STATE REP. DAVID
Bath was convicted of charges stemming from a 1991
orgy that involved making a sexually exploitative videotape featuring a 17-year-old boy. Bath had cospon-
sored the law against the sexual exploitation of minors
under which he was convicted.

IN CALIFORNIA, A SAN DIEGO COUNTY
supervisor sought to have his colleagues rename the
Africanized honeybees because he said the name has
racial overtones.

OREGON STATE REP. LIZ VAN LEEUWEN
sponsored a bill that would require each household in
the state to have on hand at least one gun and ammunition for it. Van Leeuwen introduced the bill at the
request of a gun dealer, explaining in her weekly newsletter that the media "seem surprised that regular folks
can come up with new ideas."

THE 15-MEMBER SANTA CLARA COUNTY,
California, Self-Esteem Task Force, set up to study the
effect of low self-esteem on society, disbanded in 1994.
The reason: Not enough members felt the meetings
were worth attending. In three years, the panel
reached a quorum only three times.

WHEN TAIWAN'S DEPUTY SPEAKER WANG
Chin-ping announced that the legislature would vote
on bills recognizing a top policy think tank and the
government's main spy agency without debate, opposition lawmakers responded by smashing microphones
and a voting machine with the speaker's gavel, then
throwing trash cans, chairs, water and documents at
ruling Nationalist Party legislators. Stella Chen of the
opposition Democratic Progressive Party covered the

deputy speaker's head with a trash can. The official record showed the bills passed 62–0, mainly because opponents were too busy brawling to press the buttons on their voting machines. "There is no legislature in the world that votes a bill like this," said Chen Kuei-miao of the opposition New Party.

WOMEN LEGISLATORS JOINED THE FRAY at a June 1994 session of Taiwan's National Assembly, screaming, trading slaps and kicks, and pulling each other's hair. The violence began when two members of the ruling Nationalist Party poked fun at opposition lawmaker Su Chih-yang after her underwear showed when she sat down. Nationalist lawmaker Kuo Su-chun berated Su, saying "As a woman you should also review your own behavior." Accusing Kuo of insinuating that she sat immodestly, Su walked to the podium and slapped her. Four other women joined the fracas, and a fifth collapsed from high blood pressure when she tried to stop it.

IN THE LEGISLATURE OF INDIA'S MOST populous state, Uttar Pradesh, newly elected members of the Hindu party protested the arrest of some of their party leaders before the election. When the speaker of

the house ignored their plea to adjourn the assembly
until the leaders were freed, they began ripping microphones from their desks and using them as weapons
to bludgeon fellow lawmakers, smashing glass lamps,
throwing shoes and chairs and pummeling colleagues
who cowered under their desks. At the end of the 25-
minute battle, 40 legislators and security marshals had
to be hospitalized.

TENNESSEE STATE REP. FRANK BUCK
cited a report on the death penalty that put the cost
of lethal injection at $46,000 per execution and a firing
squad at $7,000. "With figures like these, should we
wonder why people don't trust government?" he com-
mented. "I believe I can figure out a way to shoot
someone for less than $7,000."

A REPUBLICAN CAUCUS IN GRAND
Rapids, Michigan, was unable to start because no one
remembered to bring a flag for the pledge of alle-
giance. To resolve the crisis, party member Jack Pettit,
who was wearing a necktie that had a stars-and-stripes
motif, stood on a chair in front of the room while everyone placed hand on heart and recited the pledge.

TOLEDO, OHIO, MAYOR CARTY FINKBEI-
ner, noting that the agency which operates Toledo Express Airport was buying up nearby homes because jet
noise exceeds government standards, suggested that
deaf people might not be as bothered by the noise and
raised the possibility of offering them homes that others are fleeing.

CALIFORNIA ASSEMBLYMAN JOHN BUR-
ton of San Francisco introduced a bill that would
"make it a felony to intentionally and maliciously have
a yearly income below the federally established poverty level."

AFTER LOSING THE MARYLAND GOVER-
nor's race to Parris Glendening by 5,993 votes in the
November 1994 election, Ellen Sauerbrey sued to have
the results overturned. Among the votes she challenged were 37 she said were cast by dead people,
whose names she released. A spot check by *Washington Post* reporters found that at least 18 of the people
on her list were alive, including eight who said they
voted for Sauerbrey.

REPUBLICAN DON "BIG DADDY" GARLITS announced that he was running for Congress in Florida's Third Congressional District, a racially gerrymandered black enclave represented by Democrat Corrine Brown. A few days later, Garlits, who is white, announced a change of plans. According to *Campaigns & Elections* magazine, he explained that he had thought it necessary to live in the district he would represent and that he lived in the Third, but he had since discovered that he actually lived in the Sixth and that he only had to live somewhere in the same state as his prospective constituents. Therefore, he said, he was running in the Fifth, against U.S. Rep. Karen Thurman, a Democrat. Garlits lost.

MEXICO'S SECRETARY OF EDUCATION LIED about his own educational background. The Mexico City *Reforma* reported that Fausto Alzati, named to his post in December 1994, claimed to have a doctorate from Harvard University but actually never finished his postgraduate work.

RESPONDING TO A CLASS-ACTION LAW-suit filed on behalf of California's 375 prisoners facing execution, State Attorney General Dan Lungren announced a plan to prove the state's gas chambers do not inflict needless pain. Lungren proposed inserting balloons in the anuses of 60 rats, inflating them until the rats squeal, then administering cyanide gas to test the claim that the poison actually lessens pain.

AFTER BEING ELECTED TO THE DAVIS, California, City Council, Julie Partansky proposed having the crossing guard at the weekly farmers' market dress in a vegetable costume. The council rejected the request after Police Chief Phil Coleman claimed that motorists wouldn't recognize the guard's authority. "If you had a carrot directing traffic out there," he explained, "you, as a driver, wouldn't know if it was a commercial promotion or an escapee from a fruit or vegetable farm."

PEDRO JOSÉ MUÑOZ, MAYOR OF CEBRE-ros, Spain, issued a ban on running, jumping or standing still in village streets. Pedestrians must walk in single file where there are no sidewalks and keep as close as possible to buildings; they must never stop to chat; they cannot step into the road to hail a bus or taxi; and passengers are banned from stepping into or out of a moving vehicle "even if the driver agrees." Insisting that his "complimentary traffic ordinance" reflects the will of the village's 3,800 residents, Muñoz explained, "It is logical that we should ask that when people are in the streets, they should not bother the traffic or the rest of the public."

CESAR MAIA, THE MAYOR OF RIO DE JA-neiro, defied a federal government decree to end daylight saving time on January 31, 1993, by declaring that the city would remain on the summer schedule until February 28. He explained the extra hour of daylight would help the economy by giving people more daylight to go out and spend money and an extra hour at the beach. "I am not going to turn my clock back," he declared, "nor will the clocks controlled by the city be turned back."

When confusion immediately resulted because Rio's banks, businesses, airports, bus stations, stock market and major companies operated on the federal government's time, Maia relented.

ELECTION REGISTRARS IN EAST WINDSOR, Connecticut, banned political candidates from grinning within 75 feet of a polling place. Democrat Marilyn Rajala proclaimed that hanging around the polls smiling "constitutes electioneering."

WHILE RUNNING FOR CONGRESS FROM California in 1994, Sonny Bono credited an encounter on the set of the television show *Fantasy Island* in 1974 for causing him to rethink his life and enter the world of politics. According to Bono, he mistakenly addressed the late Hervé Villechaize's character Tattoo as "Pontoon." "He kicked me," said Bono. "I said, 'Thank you, God. I got the message.'"

DURING A 1995 DEBATE BY THE NORTH Carolina State House Appropriations Committee on a proposal to eliminate state funding for abortions for poor women, Republican member Henry Aldridge pronounced that rape victims don't get pregnant. "The facts show that people who are raped—who are truly raped—the juices don't flow, the body functions don't work, and they don't get pregnant," he said. "Medical authorities agree that this is a rarity, if ever."

The 71-year-old periodontist made the comments after he took the floor in an attempt to apologize for earlier remarks, which appeared to imply that rape and incest victims were sexually promiscuous.

MEMBERS OF THE ATLANTA CITY COUNCIL approved a resolution inviting Bucharest, Hungary, to become one of its sister cities. Unfortunately, Bucharest is the capital of Romania.

GUATEMALAN PRESIDENT JORGE SERrano Elias defended himself against television footage showing the born-again Christian leaving a New York City topless club by blaming leftist guerrilla "manipulation" for the alleged videotape.

MAHATHIR BIN MOHAMAD, PRIME MINISter of Malaysia, warned that too much democracy can cause homosexuality, moral decay, racial intolerance, single-parent families and a decline in the economy.

FORMER TREASURY DEPARTMENT CHIEF of Staff Joshua L. Steiner, 28, speaking before the Senate Banking Committee in 1994 concerning the Whitewater investigation: "I made no attempt to be inaccurate, but I want to be clear I was not attempting to be precise."

GERMAN LABOR MINISTER NORBERT
Blum, 59, stripped to his underwear and jumped into a harbor near Athens for a $45 dare made while drinking ouzo. The German paper *Bild* reported that Blum swam a few strokes to applause from onlookers.

3.
LIFESTYLES OF THE DUMB AND DUMBER

Chronicles of
Human Folly

SPAIN'S JOSÉ LUIS ASTOREKA CLAIMED
a world record after crushing 30 walnuts in 57 seconds
between the cheeks of his buttocks.

A GROUP OF 30 BEER DRINKERS IN PO-
land claimed a new record for the world's biggest
drinking binge after downing 104 gallons in 12 hours.
The event was organized by the Polish Beer Lovers
Party to show that beer can be enjoyed socially.

ALMOST ONE-FIFTH OF ALL MAIL RECEIVED
by the *Guinness Book of World Records* at its London
headquarters comes from India. And Indians are a
large proportion of the record holders acknowledged
by the organization. Feats such as growing the world's
largest mustache (7 feet, 10 inches), standing still the
longest (17 years), writing 1,749 letters on a grain of
rice, running backwards across the United States and
crawling the most miles (870) are all held by Indians.
"*The Guinness Book* represents recognition by the
Anglo-Saxon world, which is still highly regarded by
many people in India," said psychologist Ashis Nandy
of New Delhi. Sociologist T. K. Oommen of Jawaharlal
Nehru University added, "Indians want to know people
who are claiming distinctions, even if they only have
very long mustaches or fingernails."

AN INDIAN YOUTH IN THE CITY OF COIM-
batore, identified only by his surname, Parthasarthy,
failed at his eighty-fifth attempt to win a place in the
Guinness Book of World Records. He ate two rose
bushes in 90 minutes. He immediately announced
plans for an eighty-sixth try: eating 625 chillies. Among
Parthasarthy's previous unsuccessful attempts at recognition are swallowing 36 raw eggs and pushing a
mustard seed backwards with his nose for 1,650 feet.

INDONESIA'S MUHAMAD IKHLAS, 23, SET a record in 1995 for standing on one foot, balancing himself for 12 hours, 12 minutes and 12 seconds. In breaking his earlier mark of nine hours, two minutes and 50 seconds, Ikhlas defeated 70 contestants from Europe, Asia and Australia, many of whom blamed the tropical heat for their inability to stand on one foot for more than two hours.

HOPING TO DEMONSTRATE PERU'S changing image to the world, about 1,500 volunteers made a three-mile-long line of sardine paste sandwiches along a Lima expressway to put Peru in the *Guinness Book of World Records*. Tens of thousands of Peruvians gathered along the eight-lane highway to cheer on the group, including then–first lady Susana Higuchi de Fujimori, who declared, "This line of sandwiches represents five kilometers of Peruvian brotherhood."

AFTER SPENDING 226 DAYS LIVING UN-derground in Canon City, Colorado, retired miner Bob Leasure emerged to claim the world record. The mark turned out to be 463 days, he was informed by the *Guinness Book of World Records*, which explained that Leasure did beat the last published mark but that it had dropped the category and never published the new record in subsequent editions.

DOROLOU SWIRSKY, 83, OF SUNNYVALE, California, announced that she planned to leave the city $500,000 after her death to finance sports activities for disadvantaged youths, especially lawn bowling, which she hailed as the answer to crime and delinquency problems. "Lawn bowling is a beautiful sport," Swirsky said, explaining that it teaches children direction, discipline, manners and sportsmanship. "It embraces everything that holds a family together."

WHEN BROWARD COUNTY, FLORIDA, EN-acted a new ordinance governing X-rated entertainment, two adult businesses owned by Michael Rogers stopped their nude strip shows, changed their names and offered different services. The first, Club Romance, provided men with female dance partners, who, Rogers said, "got all their clothes on and just sit and talk to guys."

The other business, Secretaries Are Us, provided women who allow men to indulge in verbal sexual harassment for $50 a half-hour. Rogers said customers get to sit behind a desk and say whatever they want to a woman, explaining, "You can speak freely to a secretary without opening yourself up to a lawsuit." He added: "I know I can make money without someone taking their clothes off."

POLICE IN XIANGZHOU, CHINA, WHO jailed the members of two prostitution rings, said that all the women were over 70 years old, and the oldest was 93. "This is not just a moral issue," a spokesperson from the vice squad explained. "More seriously, these people are clearly contravening the terms of their pension by continuing to work."

The women reportedly worked in the city's central Fengboshan Park, servicing 200 clients a month. Pleasures included nude peeking (costing 5 yuan), bosom-touching (10 yuan) and oral sex (60 yuan, rising to 80 yuan if the client wanted the woman to remove her teeth).

INCREASING NUMBERS OF JAPANESE people are dying from golf, according to the Ministry of Health, whose study showed golf is eight times more likely than running to kill a Japanese man over 60. It ranks fourth, behind tennis, mountaineering and croquet.

Sports doctor Keizo Kogure, author of *How to Die Early by Playing Golf*, puts the fairway toll at 4,750 golfers a year. He blames stress caused by the game's status and popularity in Japan, especially among already stressed businessmen. *The Wall Street Journal* reported that one crowded public course two hours from Tokyo books players up to three months ahead and spaces foursomes just seven minutes apart. Missing a tee time could mean another three-month wait, and caddies hurry golfers along to keep them on schedule.

Adding to the stress is the pressure of trying to avoid hitting the first shot too close to the hole. A hole-in-one obligates the golfer to buy expensive gifts for his fellow players, throw a drinking party and plant a commemorative tree near the tee. Players can buy $5,000 in hole-in-one insurance before the game for about $100.

RESIDENTS OF MANGANESES DE LÁS Polvorosas in northern Spain agreed in 1993 to forgo the custom of throwing a live goat off the church bell tower at their annual festival. Instead, they reassured animal rights groups protesting the event that they would lower the animal from the 65-foot building by rope. Halfway down, however, villagers lowering the animal dropped it, and villagers below caught it in a canvas sheet.

Mayor José Manuel Gil Barrio defended the ceremony, which began in the nineteenth century after a priest locked a goat in the church belfry during a famine to prevent it from being eaten. The current priest, Honorino Gonzalez, insisted that goat-tossing had no religious significance, explaining, "People only do it for fun."

IN HONG KONG, A NEW COMPUTERIZED arm-wrestling machine broke the arms of at least five young men in video parlors in one two-week period. Arm Champs II challenges players to wrestle a silver-plated mechanized arm. Although the machine cautions players to "Play at your own risk," the signs are in English and most players are young Cantonese.

THE WONDERFUL WORLD OF DUNG, A nature study of animals' excretory habits that aired on cable television's Discovery Channel in 1994, drew 1.2 million viewers. The show's 2.0 rating was twice the usual audience, according to the Maryland–based science and nature service. "Bringing people closer to the natural world is what Discovery does best," scheduling director Steve Chesken explained, "and I'm glad we are able to oblige no matter what the topic."

IN 1987, DUTCH PIG FARMERS BEGAN AR-
ranging marriages to increase their stock of dung. In
an attempt to keep fertilizer stocks from seeping into
the water table, Holland set limits on the amount of
dung farmers can hoard. The two loopholes are to
marry the child of a pig farmer and receive dung rights
as a dowry or arrange for an engaged partner to purchase dung rights before the marriage.

TWENTY-THREE PIECES OF FOSSILIZED DI-
nosaur dung, scooped from around Hanksville, Utah,
sold for $4,500 at Bonhams, a London auction house.
Owner Jan Stobbe, a Dutch geologist, said the dung,
sold to an unidentified British buyer, brought 10 times
as much as he thought it was worth.

WHEN SCIENTISTS SENT WORD VIA A COM-
puter link to Maurizio Montalbini, 40, that his year-long
stay in an underground lab was complete, he couldn't
believe it. According to Montalbini, who kept his own
record of time, he still had a little more than six
months to go. Montalbini, 990 feet below ground, spent
his time watching videos, cultivating plants and listening to Pink Floyd.

DECLARING IT A "MATTER OF HONOR," PEdro Guattero proved friends wrong who bet him that a watermelon could not be rolled for 220 miles through the streets of Vera Cruz, Mexico.

IN AN ATTEMPT TO SOMEHOW TEACH teenagers abstinence from sex, York County, Pennsylvania, declared Monday, March 22, 1993, "The Great Sex-Out Day," asking everyone in the county to abstain from sex. "If you can control yourself for one day," Joe Fay, chairman of the Teen Pregnancy Coalition of York County, said, "you can control yourself any day."

One teen conceded that abstaining on a Monday wasn't too hard but said a Friday would be more difficult. Shoppers at a local mall also said that a sexless Monday would be do-able, "as long as it's voluntary," one 40-year-old said, "and they don't get into that 'have to' stuff."

OFFICIALS AT GREAT PARK, NEAR England's Windsor Castle, reported that a woman was treated for a broken leg after she fell naked from an oak tree while having sex. "As they reached the height of their passion, the woman slipped from one of the branches at the top of the tree and plunged to the ground," a park spokesperson explained. "It was a very clear case of coitus interruptus."

POLICE IN NEW YORK ARRESTED JIN Hyung Park and Wan Gi Jang for providing students taking the Scholastic Aptitude Test with brainy impostors to take the tests for them. Students paid $4,000 for the SAT and up to $40,000 for the Certified Public Accountant Exam.

SALES OF EGYPTIAN SINGER SABER ABU Ala's latest album soared after he was arrested for one of the bloodiest attacks on Cairo tourists in history. Abu Ala burst into the lobby of a five-star hotel and gunned down two Americans and a Frenchman. There had been little interest in the 28-year-old's music until after the attack.

A SURVEY BY THE SPECIAL REPORT NET- work that asked women whether they would prefer to watch a man dance naked or wash the dishes found that 61 percent preferred to watch him wash dishes. Also asked whether they would prefer so-so sex in a clean house or great sex in a dirty one, 53 percent of women picked the clean house.

....

FRANK GEORGI, 28, A GERMAN ENTRE-
preneur, announced plans to purchase an old army base and re-create the world of the former East Germany as a theme park. Georgi, who used to work as a tour guide and music promoter in East Germany, said he envisions a setting in which visitors would sign over most of their rights upon entering the camp for the length of their stay. Employees of the park such as waiters, bartenders or security guards will act as secret police. Guests who criticize the system they experience will be arrested and detained in jail for part of their stay. Only East German–made Trabant and Wartburg automobiles will be allowed in the park. Taxis will be the Soviet-made Volgas, just like those present in the old East Germany. The only products for sale in the park will be those that used to be available to East Germans. The only television shows available will be old East German films and political documentaries from the old state network. "Most people in West Germany and other countries never knew what life was like for us," Georgi said, "and this will be a chance for them to see."

RESEARCH FUNDED BY A BRITISH JUICE
company found that 50,000 Britons seek hospital treatment each year due to injuries caused by struggling to open milk and juice cartons.

SEVEN PEOPLE DIED IN 1993 AFTER ACCI-
dentally falling into the Grand Canyon, including Donna Spangler, 59, who fell while backing into position for a snapshot. Park officials said that they couldn't recall a worse year for falls. "A lot of tourists approach the Grand Canyon like a ride at Disneyland or some other amusement park and think it's idiot-proof," said Tom Jensen, executive director of Grand Canyon Trust, an environmental group. "The Grand Canyon wasn't built by attorneys and engineers."

SWISS MOUNTAIN RESCUE SQUADS COM-
plained that huge numbers of ill-equipped tourists were ignoring safeguards and getting stranded or killed in their attempts to climb Alpine mountains, relying on the squads to come and rescue them. Some tourists, having only so many vacation days, begin climbing even in bad weather. On good days during climbing season, as many as 150 people set out to climb the

Matterhorn. One worker complained of busloads of Eastern Europeans who "don't listen to our warnings and are brutally badly equipped." Many can't afford guides and so set out on their own, with no record of where they are going. "They get out of the cable cars and decide to take a walk in their sneakers. The weather turns bad and they're caught." Others set unreasonable goals, such as the two men who climbed up and down the Matterhorn four times in one day, each time from a different side.

IN THE SPRING OF 1993 A FRENCH– Nepalese expedition scaled Mount Everest. Its mission was to pick up between 17 and 50 tons of trash left by hundreds of climbers since the 1950s. Strewn around the mountain were ropes, tents, stoves, food containers, 20,000 empty oxygen bottles and about 20 corpses (although the former head of the Nepal Mountaineering Association estimated the body count to be more than 100). The expedition collected what they could and sent it on sleds to a base camp where it was then loaded onto yaks who took it to an airfield where it was flown away. The total cost for the mission was $740,000.

THE SCOTTISH FIRM ASSOCIATED METAL
designed and built a state-of-the-art outhouse to be installed 20,000 feet up Mount Everest. Steel ropes an-
chored with ice picks keep the toilet and its occupants
from blowing over in howling Himalayan winds. The
$10,500 privy features a wooden seat for warmth and
a lock for privacy. "Until now, climbers and Sherpas
have had to go off and find boulders and bushes to
hide behind," Phil Tolan, Associated's managing director, said. "Now, life will be a bit more comfortable,
private and clean for them."

MERCHANTS WHO OPENED BUSINESSES
at Dhaka's National Stadium, which attracts as many
as 80,000 shoppers during frequent soccer games, complained that they are running out of patience with uri-
nating fans. The six-story-high arena was built in 1960
without public toilets. "It's disgusting," electronics
merchant Hasanuzzman Moni explained. "They urinate
on shoppers from atop the stadium as if it's raining."

AUTHORITIES IN KAMPALA, UGANDA, AN-
nounced that they were hunting a man who knocks
out gorillas with tranquilizer darts, then dresses them
in clown outfits.

IN TAIWAN, DR. JUNG KAO-FANG OF Chang Gung Memorial Hospital reported that the hospital had received 82 patients, 52 of them women, suffering from "lovemaking anxiety" caused by portable phones and beepers. "The phones would ring and beepers beep in the middle of their lovemaking," Jung said. "The husbands either hurried through or stopped to run out for business appointments."

COMPETITION FOR READERS AMONG TURkey's three leading daily newspapers has prompted them several times to give away encyclopedias to boost circulation. Papers devote entire front pages to promotional announcements for single books and multivolume sets, and TV commercials tout the advantages of one paper's reference books over those of its competitors.

During one campaign, the mass-circulation *Sabah* reportedly doubled sales in one day, to two million, when it gave away a free encyclopedia with each paper. Although a fifth of Turkey's 55 million people cannot read, *Sabah* enticed illiterates to buy papers by offering cars and color television sets.

IN FEBRUARY 1994, CBS TELEVISED THE
story of Cecil B. Jacobson, a Virginia fertility doctor
who from 1976 to 1988 told women they were being
inseminated with sperm from anonymous donors with
physical characteristics resembling their husbands, but
who actually used his own sperm. In the made-for-TV
movie, *Babymaker*, Melissa Gilbert starred as the
mother of one of the 75 children believed to have been
fathered by Jacobson. "Anything bizarre makes a good
movie of the week now," said Dr. John Doppelheuer,
the obstetrician-gynecologist who first reported Jacobson to the Virginia Board of Medicine. "People with
serious personality disorders can always get on TV."

WHEN BASHIR ZEGLAN, 37, BECAME A
U.S. citizen in Fort Worth, Texas, in 1993, he officially
changed his name to Clint Eastwood. "He's my hero,"
the Libyan-born used-car dealer explained, adding, "My
brother laughed, but so what? When he got his citizen-
ship, he took the name Mike White. How boring."

MARYLAND STATE POLICE ASSIGNED TWO
mannequins donated by a Baltimore–area clothing
store to sit in the driver's seat of old patrol cars along

a busy interstate highway, hoping speeders would think they were real troopers and slow down. When they began getting calls from people wondering if something bad had happened to the stiff-looking trooper, the police put a sign in the car window informing motorists that the occupant wasn't a real trooper.

IN CLEVELAND, ENGLAND, HELEN STEphens, 20, was sentenced to a week in jail for harassing her neighbors by playing her Whitney Houston record, "I Will Always Love You," continuously for six weeks. Witnesses testified Stephens played the song so loudly that it penetrated a double brick wall, insulation and several wardrobes and shook her neighbor's floorboards.

IN THE BANGLADESH VILLAGE OF SAVAR, a monkey on a rampage hospitalized at least 13 people. The monkey entered homes and showed consistent behavior on encountering different types of people: it slapped children, bit women and scratched men. While vigilante groups and police looked for it to kill it, a youth group called "Youth for Animals" staged demonstrations in support of the monkey. Fifty college students at one street protest chanted, "You have nothing

to fear. We are with you," while carrying signs reading
WE ARE READY TO DIE FOR THE FREEDOM OF THE MONKEY.

AFTER A MOUNTAIN LION ATTACKED AND
killed a marathon runner in California's Sierra foot-
hills, a trust fund was set up for the woman's two children. After authorities tracked and killed the lion,
another fund was established for the lion's orphaned
cub. When the cub's fund had reached $21,000 in just
weeks, the children's trust held only $9,000.

ANTONY HICKS, A RABID BRITISH FAN OF
the rock band Level 42, changed his name to include
the group's lineup and its album titles. Hicks is now
legally known as "Ant Level Forty Two The Pursuit Of
Accidents The Early Tapes Standing In The Light True
Colors A Physical Presence World Machine Running In
The Family Running In The Family Platinum Edition
Staring At The Sun Level Best Guaranteed The Re-
mixes Forever Now Influences Changes Mark King
Mike Lindup Phil Gould Boon Gould Wally Badarou
Lindup-Badarou."

GEORGE AND TINA ROLLASON OF YORK, Pennsylvania, named their daughter Atheist Evolution Rollason. Said George: "There's so many people named Christian, or Christine. This is just one person named Atheist. What the heck's the difference?"

A BLACK FEMALE STUDENT AT THE UNI-versity of Pennsylvania was asked to leave a meeting of the group White Women Against Racism because she was black. Elena DiLapi, director of the Women's Center, a sponsor of the event, said later that the group believes racism "is a white problem and we have a responsibility as white women in particular to do what we can to eradicate racism."

POLICE IN SAUGERTIES, NEW YORK, AR-rested 32-year-old Kathy Bowen of Bristol, Pennsylvania, for trespassing after she refused to leave the site of the 1994 Woodstock festival a full three days after the show ended.

IN OHIO, A SMALL PLANE CRASH-LANDED
on the runway at Toledo Express Airport. It went un-
noticed for 30 minutes, even by the control tower, until
one of the three occupants finally hiked to the airport's
main terminal and reported the mishap to United Express employees.

IN CALIFORNIA, MORE THAN 600 PEOPLE
were taking the State Bar exams in the Pasadena Convention Center when a 50-year-old man taking the test
suffered a seizure. Only two other test takers stopped
to help the man, John Leslie and Eunice Morgan. They
administered CPR until paramedics arrived, then resumed taking the exam. Citing policy, the test supervisor refused to allow the two additional time to make
up for the 40 minutes they spent helping the victim.
Jerome Braun, the State Bar's senior executive for ad-
missions, backed the decision.

AFTER A COURT ATTENDANT IN SYRA-
cuse, New York, swore in a witness in a murder trial,
she realized that instead of a Bible, she had used another book that was on the same table: a romance
novel by Danielle Steele.

IN A DIVORCE CASE IN HENDERSONVILLE,
Tennessee, Carol Ann Bennett asked Circuit Judge
Thomas Goodall to award her custody of her breast
implants. Noting that her estranged husband, Warren
Woodrow Bennett Jr., had the implants, she explained
that she had had them removed after contracting lupus
but left them behind when she moved out of their con-
dominium. She told the judge that she wanted them
for a lawsuit against their manufacturer but feared
Warren would destroy them. "Divorce granted to
wife," Goodall ruled, "breasts to be returned to wife."

INTENT ON TRUMPING FRENCH CUISINE,
Swiss chef Leon Marmy announced the creation of
"foie d'escargot," the world's first liver-of-snail dish.
The delicacy costs $30 a plate, and one pound of
moussed snail livers requires 2,000 snails.

THE 23 LAWYERS WHO FORMED RODNEY
King's legal team submitted a bill to the city of Los
Angeles for $4.4 million. The amount is $600,000 more
than the $3.8 million King received in his judgment
against the city. "All I'm asking for is a day's wage for

a day's work," Steven A. Lerman, one of the lawyers said.

Included in the 13,000 hours of work at $350 an hour was the time lawyers spent on talk shows, taking King to movie and theater premieres, attending his birthday party, trying to counter the negative publicity generated when King, with a transvestite prostitute in his car, reportedly tried to run down a police officer, and coaching him for the news conference where he pleaded, "Can we all get along?"

ONE HUNDRED PEOPLE PAID $29 TO AT-tend a spoon-bending seminar conducted by Diana Gazes, who told them that their powers of concentration would "cause an alteration in the spin of the atoms" of the spoon, according to the *San Francisco Chronicle*. To achieve success, Gazes told the audience to grasp the spoon in both hands with thumbs underneath the smallest part of the handle and "apply some downward strength." Noting that spoons handled this way bend fairly easily, the paper reported that Gazes shouted "Bend! Bend!" as the believers jumped to their feet, one by one, waving spoons and shouting, "I bent!"

Business

THE HONG KONG STOCK EXCHANGE CENsured and fined the Great Honest Investment brokerage firm for charging clients less than the exchange's minimum 0.25 percent commission on transactions. After announcing the $1,900 fine, the exchange printed the censure in Hong Kong newspapers, explaining that Great Honest's generous conduct was "injurious to the character and interests and prejudicial to the objects of the exchange."

AMONG THE 11 BRANDS OF CRAYONS THAT the Consumer Product Safety Commission recalled in 1994 because they contain lead was "Safe 48 Non-

Toxic I'm a Toys 'R' Us Kid! Crayons," distributed by the Toys "R" Us chain. The CPSC said that despite the reassuring name, the particular brand was one of three that "contain enough lead to present a lead poisoning hazard to young children who might eat or chew on the crayons."

AFTER NATIONAL PUBLIC RADIO REported the existence of a top-secret list of 599 chemicals that U.S. cigarette companies add to cigarettes, including 13 chemicals that are so toxic they are not allowed in food, the six leading tobacco companies released the list, claiming redemption because it showed they add only eight of those chemicals, not 13, to their cigarettes.

THE SWEDISH NEWSPAPER EXPRESSEN gave $1,250 each to five stock analysts and a chimp to see who could make the most money on stock market investments in 30 days. At the end of the contest Ola, the chimpanzee, was declared the winner with a total of $190 in profits.

THE FEDERAL OCCUPATIONAL SAFETY AND Health Administration cited the Pro-Line Cap Company for having too few toilet facilities for its women employees and told it to rectify the situation. The Fort Worth manufacturer of athletic caps fired 30 female workers. "We had two choices: to add toilets we could not afford or reduce the work force," said Pro-Line attorney Franklin Sears, noting that adding the required facilities would have cost $25,000. "Adding toilets would take up needed production space, and we would have to lay off anyway even if we spent the money to comply with OSHA guidelines. Since the problem concerned only females, the only corrective action to take involved only females."

CITING THE EXPANDED ROLE OF ITS MEMbers, the 41-year-old trade group International Business Forms Industries Incorporated changed its name to the International Association Serving Forms, Information Management, Systems Automation and Printed Communications Requirements of Business.

FIVE GROUPS IN THE UNITED STATES, Britain and Australia announced that they were teaming up to develop the world's first supersonic automobile. One participating engineer told London's *Sunday Times* that their goal is "one of the most extraordinary ventures in engineering today." He admitted, however, that it lacks any real purpose.

RELIEF SUPPLIES DONATED BY U.S. CORporations to victims of a 1993 earthquake in India's rural Maharashtra state included dental floss, contact-lens cleaner and lubricants for sexual intercourse.

THE PHOENIX, A NEWSPAPER IN PHOENIXville, Pennsylvania, reported the arrest of a man accused of sexually abusing his teenage daughter, noting twice that it was withholding the man's name to protect his children's identity. According to the *Columbia Journalism Review*, the story was accompanied by a 4-by-6-inch color photo of the family's house and a caption naming the street it's on.

CONCERNED THAT PEOPLE INTENDING TO rent a video might get confused and order a pizza instead, Blockbuster Entertainment sued a pizzeria in

Fort Lauderdale, Florida, for calling itself Buster Blocks.

AFTER LAYING OFF AT LEAST 800 STAFF-ers as a cost-cutting measure, the National Geographic Society spent $220,000 to replace live yew plants outside its Washington, D.C., headquarters with artificial ones. "Our preference would certainly have been to maintain live plants. We tried for ten years," Geographic spokesperson Barbara Fallon said, explaining that the real yew plants had died due to soil and drainage problems.

WHEN PEOPLE LIVING NEAR HONG KONG Stadium objected to a planned rock concert because of the noise, concert organizers offered to accommodate them by handing out 17,500 pairs of gloves to audience members to muffle their applause.

CAIRO'S AL AHRAM NEWSPAPER PROMI-nently published a letter to the editor protesting a Rasha-brand cookie commercial on Egyptian television in which Adolf Hitler sits on a cannon rubbing the cookies to his cheek and chanting, "I love Rasha." Letter writer Dr. Mahmoud el Sheeti complained because the commercial ridiculed the Nazi dictator. "Millions of Egyptians who remember World War II are dismayed by an advertisement which makes fun of one of this century's immortal politicians," Sheeti wrote, recalling that Egyptians had "supported the Germans with their hearts."

WALT DISNEY COMPANY, THWARTED IN

its effort to build a Virginia theme park to celebrate American history, ran ads promoting its movie *Jefferson in Paris* that credited Thomas Jefferson with writing the U.S. Constitution. An unnamed Disney executive told *Newsweek* that after the ads ran, "we all walked in Monday morning and said, 'Oh, fuck, it should have been the Declaration of Independence.'"

THE CHARTERHOUSE HOTEL IN HONG

Kong installed karaoke machines in 34 of its rooms so guests can sing to themselves.

IN AN ATTEMPT TO LESSEN GANG VIO-
lence, business leaders in Denver announced the creation of Operation Reconstruction. They said the
program would equip street gang members with
cellular phones and pay them cash to patrol their
neighborhoods and contact the police when trouble
erupted.

DURING A NEW DELHI PRIVATE BUS COM-
pany's first 10 months, its drivers were involved in 67
fatal traffic accidents and received more than 35,000
traffic tickets. The Red Line was launched after a study
showed that the government-run bus company was losing $66 million a year and failing to provide frequent
enough service for the city's 9.7 million residents. The
problem, according to *The Washington Post*, is that
each of the 2,400 Red Line buses has a different
owner. "These drivers have no fixed timetables, and
they're in competition with one another," said P. Ka-
maraj, Delhi's deputy police commissioner for traffic.
"Since profit is the main motive, they throw all safety
norms to the wind and pay scant attention to traffic
rules."

THE PACIFIC STOCK EXCHANGE AN-
nounced a crackdown on horseplay among traders,
which increased during a period of slow trading. Michael A. Barth, director of floor operations, warned
that any trader caught shooting rubber bands, spitballs
or other projectiles would be fined $1,000 for a first
offense and $5,000 for third-time offenders.

A COCA-COLA PROMOTION IN NICARAGUA,
offering $8,250 to people with a certain number printed
inside a Coke bottle cap, backfired when a local newspaper misprinted the winning number. About 3,000
people tried to claim the prize. When the company refused to pay, hundreds of winners mobbed a Coca-
Cola bottling plant and threatened to burn it down.

COURTS IN THE PHILIPPINES BEGAN
hearing civil and criminal cases filed against Pepsi Cola
in the wake of another lucky bottle cap promotion
gone awry. When Pepsi announced 349 as the winning
number, thousands of people rushed to Pepsi plants
around the country to collect their $37,000 prize. The
company refused to pay, explaining that the bottle
caps with the winning number didn't also have the cor-

rect security number. The winners countered that contest literature didn't mention anything about a security code. Pepsi officials said that as a "goodwill gesture," they would pay $20 to anyone holding one of the 800,000 caps with the number 349. The company, which had budgeted $2 million for the whole four-month-long promotion, paid out $10 million, but irate winners rioted at some bottling plants and attacked plants and delivery trucks with grenades and fire-bombs. About 50,000 of the cap holders organized as the "349 Alliance" to pursue further claims.

Pepsi officials blamed the flap on "a computer software glitch," but a Philippine senate committee accused Pepsi of "gross negligence." It noted that the company was involved in a similar fiasco in Chile just a month before the 349 incident when a garbled fax transmission led to a wrong number being announced on television.

HOOVER OFFERED ITS BRITISH AND IRISH customers two free air tickets worth up to $600 with each vacuum cleaner purchase of more than $150. Sales rose, requiring the company to go on overtime to produce enough vacuums. Then 200,000 people applied for tickets. Hoover couldn't meet the demand. Admitting the promotion was not well thought out (it had expected customers to pick up tickets as an afterthought, not buy the cheaper cleaners to get tickets), Hoover's parent, the Maytag Corporation, announced the gaffe would cost the company $30 million.

THE ARKANSAS AUTOMOBILE DEALERS
Association voted 285–0 to recommend that the state
legislature require them to be closed on Sundays, even
though no law forces them to be open.

BRITISH RAIL ANNOUNCED PLANS TO HAR-
ness some of its employees to posts six to nine feet
from railroad tracks to determine how close maintenance workers could safely work to trains traveling up
to 140 mph. No BR workers volunteered, but, according to a spokesperson, more than 50 members of the
public called to offer their services, including one
caller who termed the experiment "the railway equiv-
alent of bungee jumping."

GERMAN POLICE ARRESTED MORE THAN
60 people involved in a telephone sex ring. The suspects reportedly obtained large sums from telephone
companies for providing a service that tricked callers
into spending $260 million a year thinking they were
talking live to telephone sex partners. Actually, up
to 80 percent of the so-called conversations were
prerecorded.

VOLVO GM HEAVY TRUCK CORPORATION

in Dublin, Virginia, assigned an employee to dress up as a rooster, sneak up behind tardy workers and crow. When the rooster surprised Marshall Lineberry, 50, who was three hours late for his shift, and yelled "cock-a-doodle-do," Lineberry turned around, grabbed the rooster and began choking it. Volvo GM suspended Lineberry, who filed for unemployment. The employment commission denied him benefits, citing "misconduct in connection with work." Pulaski Circuit Court Judge Colin Gibb overruled the panel, finding that the rooster's act amounted to provocation.

Medicine and Science

A CLINIC OPENED IN BERGEN, NORWAY, that is exclusively for patients who are in good health. It treats hypochondriacs. Clinic psychiatrist Ingvard Wilhelmsen explained that since hypochondriacs spend so much time worrying about their imaginary illnesses, "they really do suffer."

WARNING THAT IF AMERICANS KEEP growing at the same rate as they have for the past 75 years, the environmental consequences could be devastating, San Diego researcher Thomas T. Samaras said that the solution is smaller people. Just growing another 20 percent taller, for instance, will increase energy needs by 50 percent, require an additional 180 million acres for food production and add 3 billion tons of carbon dioxide to the atmosphere, according to his book, *The Truth About Your Height*. "Carefully monitoring the diet of children, and I don't mean starving them, can restrict height by as much as eight inches," 5-foot-10 Samaras suggested. "The Earth would be better off if people were shorter. An average height of five feet and a weight of around a hundred and ten pounds would be about right."

BRITISH SCIENTISTS SEEKING TO CREATE an authentic jungle habitat in "Butterfly World" released two 18-month-old cotton-eared marmosets into the huge glass-enclosed houses, home to 3,000 butterflies from 60 species. Within a week, the marmosets, whose diet consists of fruit and nuts, devoured more than 50 butterflies, including six Charaxes, a species near extinction.

A BRAWLEY, CALIFORNIA, MEDICAL COMpany, Clinicas de Salud Del Pueblo Incorporated, announced that workers who display hickeys would be sent home without pay and could return only when the telltale marks of passion disappear or are covered up. Personnel manager Diana Tamex explained that the company implemented the rule in response to complaints from colleagues and patients at the company's three health care clinics.

According to Dr. Mark Goulston, assistant clinical professor of psychiatry at UCLA, the small marks can lead to large fantasies. "Someone with a low sex drive may look at it as a bruise," he said. "Someone with a lot of sex on their mind will look at a hickey as if they're watching Sharon Stone in *Basic Instinct*."

THE PRINCETON DENTAL RESOURCE CENTer in Albany, New York, agreed to pay a $25,000 settlement for misleading consumers by claiming that a piece of chocolate a day might inhibit tooth decay. The center is funded by candy maker Mars Incorporated.

A HOSPITAL IN BIRMINGHAM, ENGLAND, rented out a sophisticated cancer scanner to help farmers breed sheep and pigs. Noting the $750,000 mobile scanner was used to check fat and muscle content of potential breeding stock only when no patients were scheduled to use it, hospital manager Robert Naylor defended his action as a sensible way to raise money for cash-strapped health services.

AFTER NOTICING A LARGE MUSHROOM growing in the roots of a fallen tree in her yard in West Point, Indiana, Virginia Emerick carefully mowed around it until it was two-feet wide and weighed 40 pounds. Then she harvested it and presented it to Purdue University's plant and fungi collection to be dried and used as an educational specimen. When it turned out to be too wide to fit in the special dryer, three of the school's scientists sauteed it in butter and ate it.

AFTER AUSTRALIAN GASTROENTEROLO-gist Terry Bolin urged people to avoid flatulence-producing turkey and plum pudding at Christmas to reduce methane emissions and help save the ozone layer, Professor Tom Wigley of the climate research unit at the University of East Anglia in England explained that methane doesn't destroy ozone. "Methane increases the amount of ozone, and so the more you fart—if you can get it up there into the stratosphere—the better it is for the ozone layer," he said. "For the ozone layer, fart as much as you possibly can."

Wigley backed up his assertion, noting that he worked over Christmas to calculate "the greenhouse effect of extra farts." He said the effect of a billion people (his estimate of the Christian population celebrating Christmas) emitting two liters more methane a day for seven days would increase methane output by

0.00002 percent, enough to raise temperatures "about a hundred-thousandth of a degree Celsius."

A WILMINGTON, NORTH CAROLINA, NEU-rosurgeon's license was suspended for five months after he was accused of leaving a patient's brain exposed for 25 minutes while he ate lunch. No other physician was present to care for the patient, according to the state medical board, which said that on other occasions Dr. Raymond Sattler, 50, forgot the names of surgical equipment during an operation, told a nurse to drill holes in a patient's head and work on his outer brain even though she wasn't trained to do so, and ordered intravenous fluid to be given to him while performing surgery because he thought he was going to pass out.

THE MEDICAL BOARD OF CALIFORNIA charged Dr. Fereydoune Shirazi, 55, with leaving the operating room for 11 minutes during surgery on a man's back to make a phone call and use the bathroom. The board said that Shirazi, who was using a foot pedal–activated cutting tool, placed a sandbag on the pedal, keeping the blades of the device rotating in the man's spinal column while he was out of the room.

UNIVERSITY HOSPITAL IN STONY BROOK,
New York, suspended Dr. Michael J. Swango from his
position as a resident in psychiatry after learning that
he had been sent to prison for feeding ant poison to
six paramedics in Illinois and investigated for suspicious patient deaths in Ohio. The Illinois prosecutor
who sent him to prison described Swango as a charm-
ing "psychopath" who "likes to experiment on people."

DR. MAURICE NELLIGAN, ONE OF IRE-
land's leading heart surgeons, blamed a successful
campaign by police to reduce drunk driving for a de-
crease in the number of organs available for emergency transplants.

A BRITISH MURDER INVESTIGATION WAS
delayed for two and a half days after a doctor and a
police inspector examined a dead body discovered in
a bedroom and decided that it was a case of death by
natural causes, despite the presence of blood on the
man's face, clothes and on the carpet and walls of the
room. Only after the body was taken to a mortuary did
an attendant notice five bullet wounds in the corpse's
head, including one in the forehead. "How the doctor

---

missed that I don't know," said prosecutor Michael Nelligan.

POPPY FALDMO, 21, OF SALT LAKE CITY was unable to afford a tonsillectomy, so she removed her own tonsils. She reportedly spent hours every day in front of a mirror, using nail scissors and a small knife to cut out the inflamed tonsils a bit at a time, using a toothache gel as an anesthetic.

IN INDIA, SOME 150,000 ASTHMA SUF-ferers flock to Hyderabad each spring to swallow live sardines to relieve their condition. An herbal concoction is placed in the sardine's mouth. The sufferer swallows the fish, repeating the treatment every 15 days.

Skool Daze

Two students who failed a Japanese university entrance exam won admission to the school after complaining that they couldn't hear the questions over the supervisor's snoring. A spokesperson for the Kobe City University of Foreign Studies explained that the test consisted of English comprehension questions relayed by loudspeaker and that a number of students insisted the broadcast was inaudible because of snoring and noseblowing in the room. "I didn't fall asleep," the supervisor said, "but I wasn't feeling very well and my nose might have been making some noise."

PARENTS IN GASTON COUNTY, NORTH
Carolina, demanded that Africa and Germany be removed from maps in school classrooms, charging that
those places are anti-Christian. They also said that
teaching the Greek alphabet constitutes an endorse-
ment of homosexuality.

TEACHERS AND ADMINISTRATORS ASKED
the Weymouth, Massachusetts, school board to require
intermediate school students to applaud performances
by fellow students. "If you get a ten-year-old girl who's
singing her heart out," Principal Christine Collins said,
"we'd like to see the children clapping, whether she's
good or not."

IN INDIA'S BIHAR STATE, UNIVERSITY STU-
dents rioted, demanding the right to cheat on their examinations. After being denied permission to bring
their notes into the examination hall, students set fire
to railroad stations, police stations and government
buildings before police opened fire, wounding about a
dozen rioters and killing one.

SIX GIRLS AT OREGON'S SILVERTON HIGH
School who were chosen for a pep rally stunt to see who could sit on a block of dry ice the longest suffered severe burns on their buttocks. Dry ice is solid carbon dioxide and can be as cold as 112 degrees below zero. Several of the students may need skin grafts, according to Dr. Frank Lord of Silverton Hospital, who noted, "The truth is, I've never seen any frostbite on this part of the anatomy."

IN COLOMBIA, ANTANAS MOKUS, PRESI-
dent of Bogotá's National University, was speaking at the opening of an art exhibition when a group of students began heckling him. Mokus acknowledged them by turning around, lowering his pants and underwear and bending over. He explained afterward that the incident, which was recorded by a student on videotape and broadcast on national television, should be understood "as a part of the resources that an artist can use."

A 1992 REVIEW OF 10 U.S. HISTORY TEXT-
books uncovered about 5,200 historical inaccuracies. Among the bloopers: General Douglas MacArthur, not

Joe McCarthy, led the anti-Communist crusade of the 1950s; President Truman "easily settled" the Korean War, not World War II, by dropping "the bomb"; the wrong date was given for the Japanese attack on Pearl Harbor.

IN 1990 *FACTS ON FILE* ASKED LIBRARIans to return copies of the *Junior Visual Dictionary* by J. C. Corbeil so that they could correct the misidentified anatomical drawing of the female body that it contained. The female's vagina had been labeled "sex."

THE 1993 EDITION OF THE IOWA STATE University yearbook, *The Bomb*, sold only 1,500 copies. Someone had mistakenly labeled the section on the campus's Greek system as "Geek."

JANE BROWN, THE HEADMISTRESS OF A London school, declined a charity's offer of cut-price tickets for all of her school's students under the age of 11 to attend the ballet of *Romeo and Juliet* on the stage of London's Covent Garden ballet and opera house. According to local officials, Brown said that until books, film and the theater reflected all forms of sexuality, she would not involve her students in heterosexual culture. They related that she described *Romeo and Juliet* as a blatantly heterosexual love story. Her superior described Brown's decision as "ideological idiocy and cultural philistinism."

A WISCONSIN ELEMENTARY SCHOOL CUS-todian was suspended without pay for 30 days after he was discovered working nude in the building on the weekend.

A SCHOOL BUS DRIVER IN MERIDEN, CON-necticut, tried to discipline rowdy elementary school students, ranging from five to 10 years in age, by closing all the windows on the bus, turning up the heat (it was May) and driving in circles while yelling obscenities at them for 15 minutes.

MILWAUKEE ATTORNEY DEBRA KOENIG, speaking to a class of seventh graders on the topic of women in the workplace, told the students, "I think it's great not to get married until after you finish your education . . . Frankly, sleep around all you want, but don't get married."

HALF MOON BAY, CALIFORNIA, SCHOOL board member Garrett Redmond proposed a ban on homework for students. "Homework is burning students out terribly," he said. "It interrupts family life."

MISSOURI ASSISTANT ATTORNEY GEN- eral Erich Vieth got a court order to bar the International Commission for Schools from issuing any future college accreditations in the state after it granted one to a fictitious school created by the Attorney General's office. Vieth's office had asked the commission to accredit Eastern Missouri Business College, a college they described as granting doctorates through the mail in fields such as marine biology, genetic engineering and aerospace science. College faculty included "Arnold Ziffel," the name of the pig on the old *Green Acres* television show; "Edward J. Haskell" from *Leave It to*

Beaver; and M. Howard, Jerome Howard and Lawrence Fine—the Three Stooges. The college seal in Latin read *Solum Pro Avibus Est Educatio* and *Latrocinia Et Raptus*, loosely translated as "Education is for the birds" and "Everything from petty theft to highway robbery."

Commission president George Reuter Jr. responded by pointing out, "The attorney general made a big deal out of the fact I didn't know who the Three Stooges were. Well, we've been to about two movies in the last five years, and we don't know Latin."

A LAWYER FOR THE FAMILY OF FIRST-grader Austin Scroggins said that the boy's first-grade teacher at a North Little Rock, Arkansas, elementary school sought to punish the child for leaving his desk by forcing him to crawl around on the classroom floor for an hour. According to the lawyer, the seven-year-old had gotten down on his knees to retrieve a fallen pencil when the teacher, Betty Davis, told him that he would spend the last hour of the day crawling on the floor. As he crawled, classmates called him a dog and barked at him and his knees were rubbed raw by his blue jeans.

DURING FEBRUARY 1991'S OBSERVATION of Black History Month, a Greenville, North Carolina, elementary school teacher instructed her pupils that Rosa Parks, who helped spark the civil rights movement by refusing to give up her bus seat in Montgomery, Alabama, in 1955, was actually the person responsible for assassinating Martin Luther King, Jr. When students later wrote papers on black history that were subsequently offered to the local newspaper for publication, nine out of 17 students identified Parks as the assassin.

IN 1992 RUMORS GREW AT MILFORD (Utah) High School that there was a list of students in grades nine through 12 indicating which were sexually active and which remained virgins. After being persuaded by students, a teacher actually produced the list and shared it with her classes. She was immediately suspended.

IN AN ATTEMPT TO TEACH A GROUP OF jobless women how important it is to love one's body, Swedish high school teacher Irene Wachenfeldt, 44, took off her clothes in the classroom. "My body is good enough; I want you to feel the same about your bodies," she told the class. After school officials forced her to resign, students protested. One letter declared, "It was one of our best lessons."

A 45-YEAR-OLD SIXTH-GRADE TEACHER IN Chicago presented his 30 students with a test titled "City of Chicago High School Proficiency Exam." It featured eight math problems involving selling cocaine, drive-by shootings and prison life. One read: "Rufus is pimping three girls. If the price is $65 for each trick, how many tricks will each girl have to turn so Rufus can pay for his $800-per-day crack habit?" Another asked how many more years a paroled hitman would have to serve in prison for "killing the bitch that spent his money?" Yet another read: "José has two ounces of cocaine and sells an eight ball to Jackson for $320, and two grams to Billy Joe for $85 per gram. What is the street value of the balance if he doesn't cut it?" Amid a firestorm of angry parents, the teacher reportedly offered to quit but said that he thought the test might have been a method of trying to relate to his students, according to one parent.

FIFTEEN INDONESIAN SCHOOLGIRLS ON A biology field trip drowned when their teacher forced them into the fast-flowing Opak River near Yogyakarta after no one would admit to passing gas.

ACTING ON A TIP THAT STUDENTS TAKING
an army entrance exam at Ramkhamhaeng University
would be using high-tech cheating devices, Thai police
searched more than 10,000 applicants and arrested 75
students whom they found wearing diapers equipped
with battery-operated radio receivers. Each reportedly
paid $1,800 to have answers transmitted.

Art Schmart

AT AN AUCTION IN NEW YORK CITY IN
1993, an autographed photo of former Presidents Ford,
Carter and Nixon sold for $275. A photograph signed
by Three Stooges Larry, Moe and Curly brought $1,870.

TO COMMEMORATE WHERE THE FIRST
killer bees entered the United States from Mexico in
October 1990, the city of Hidalgo, Texas, spent $20,000
to build a 20-foot-long fiberglass and steel statue,
dubbed the "World's Largest Killer Bee." "There are a
lot of wacky roadside attractions around the U.S.,"
said Joe Vera III, president of the city's chamber of
commerce. "Now we're one of them."

TO MAKE A COMMENT ON MATERIALISM, Chinese-born artist Jian Jun Xi carefully arranged money around the floor of an art gallery at London's Goldsmith College. Light-fingered art fans helped themselves to $155, prompting him to don a security uniform and recruit friends to protect the remaining $1,714.

CALIFORNIA ARTIST NICOLINO ANNOUNCED plans to collect 10,000 bras and string them up across the Grand Canyon, using large construction helicopters to drape a structural steel cable one mile across the canyon, then attaching the bras to the cable and pulling it across the canyon like underwear on a clothesline to create a bra bridge. "It's about the puritanical obsession with the breast," Nicolino said. "It's about breast implants and victimizing the health of women. It's about connecting a woman's self-identity to the size of her breasts." He embarked on a nationwide tour to collect brassieres but had to abandon the project when he couldn't get a permit.

THREE ARTISTS PAINTED A HERD OF WYoming cattle with words from the journal of Phyllis Luman Metal, an early settler who wrote about a woman's plight in the West in the early 1900s. "Cows are great and so are women. Their lives are about self-sacrifice and motherhood," said artist Sue Thornton. The project was sponsored by a $4,000 grant from the Rockefeller Foundation.

JIM ROSE, LEADER OF THE JIM ROSE CIR-
cus Sideshow, had to postpone the start of a 33-city tour in 1993 after he ate too many light bulbs and collapsed. Rose, who reportedly eats light bulbs as part of his act, said, "I ended up eating, like, five [in a] day. Normally I only eat, like, one a day. I'm doing absolutely no shows right now. I'm not being a wimp. It's just that sometimes you have to put your foot down and think of yourself." Rose said that he would recuperate by eating "like, twenty bananas and [doing] stomach exercises."

Besides eating light bulbs, Rose's act features him crawling across broken glass on stage, stapling a $5 bill to his forehead, shoving a long nail into his left nostril and acting as a human dart board as his wife throws darts into his back. Rose points out that a lot of preparation goes into his act. He carefully studies the piles of broken glass to avoid sharp edges. "I probably know more about lying in broken glass than anyone on earth," he said.

THE DALLAS GROCERY CHAIN MINYARD'S pulled the November 1993 issue of *Discover* magazine from its shelves because of the cover photo of a sculpture of two apes, the 3.2-million-year-old *Australopithecus afarensis*, with their genitals exposed. The apes are believed to be our earliest ancestors. "When it shows the genitals or the breasts," Minyard's president Jay L. Williams said, "we're going to pull it."

AN ETCHING BY FRENCH IMPRESSIONIST Pierre-Auguste Renoir, conservatively valued at about $23,000, turned up in an Australian country town, gathering dust on a filing cabinet some 40 years after it was donated to now-defunct Wagga Wagga Agricultural College as a pig-breeding trophy.

THE NETHERLANDS' FOUNDATION OF THE Museum of Silence opened an exhibition featuring 75 years of great silences from Dutch radio and television. The silent moments, on loan from the Museum of Broadcasting in Hilversum, are played to visitors over loudspeakers in the Museum of Silence. Curator Bob Vrakking said he started the foundation in 1990 to promote silence "because it is so scarce."

BRITISH ARTIST MICHAEL RUNDELL CRE-
ated a work consisting of vials of smallpox, polio, ra-
bies, herpes, yellow fever and two strains of influenza,
each frozen in pink embalming fluid and arranged on
plinths in the Museum of Ethnography in St. Peters-
burg, Russia. Armed Russian soldiers were assigned to
guard the display.

The other part of the artwork consists of a maze of
clothes arranged in the form of the DNA helix. Those
wishing to take part in the exhibit must first sign a
form stating that they understand the inherent danger
of the exhibit and then are allowed to find their way
through the maze. "The maze demonstrates that at the
center of life is the kernel of death—the seed of de-
struction," Rundell said. "From the balcony above, you
can look down on the people moving around like living
molecules, but at the very center are the viruses which
have the ability to destroy us all."

AS PART OF AN ART PROJECT TITLED "A
Celebration of Being Human," Yoko Ono had posters
plastered all over Langenhagen, Germany, which featured an unidentified derrière. She described it as "a
really nice average bum." As well as hanging from
walls, the poster was reprinted on shopping bags and
postcards. "Faces can lie. Backsides can't," said Ono.
"People talk about my pictures. . . . So long as they

continue talking about butts, they will not be killing each other."

INSPIRED BY A FIRE AT HIS SHOWROOM, clothes designer Marcos Egas began selling shirts with singed collars, pockets and cuffs. As other designers joined the trend, Haysun Hahn of the Promostyl fashion consulting agency noted that the best-looking burned garments are the ones that were really burned by hand and not fakes that try to achieve the same look by use of dyes.

SPEAKING AT A MEETING WITH THE LOCAL Kiwanis Club, Richard Muhlberger, the new director of the Knoxville, Tennessee, Museum of Art, volunteered his definition of the difference between pornography and art: "One, you get a hard-on when you look at it."

FOR NEARLY 30 YEARS, EXPERTS IN EN-gland agreed that two busts uncovered in a garden in Fence, Lancashire, and displayed at the Pendle Heritage Center were examples of ancient Celtic stonecraft. In 1994, the heads were identified as caricatures of Hitler and Mussolini, carved in 1939 by Leslie Ridings, who died in 1944. His brother Ted explained, "The heads ended up at our mother's house, and when I sold the place to the late Mr. Roger Preston in 1966 I was so busy that I forgot to clear it out properly. I forgot all about the heads until I found them in a local history book."

Sons of Flubber

NELSON CAMUS, AN ARGENTINE-BORN electrical engineer in Hacienda Heights, California, announced the invention of a battery powered by urine. Camus said that his battery generates more power than standard acid-reaction batteries and is cheaper. His partner, Ed Aguayo, said 10 urine-powered batteries, each about half the size of a normal car battery, could power a normal home.

A GERMAN COMPANY UNVEILED A NEW form of contraception for men. A small capsule implanted into both seminal ducts uses an electrical current to kill sperm before they leave a man's body. Neue

Technologien said its Contraceptive Capsule requires no outside energy source. It contains a galvanized element that causes the seminal fluid to act as an electrolyte, killing the sperm when they swim over it.

AS PART OF NORWAY'S "SMILE—YOU'RE a Tourist Attraction" campaign for the 1994 Winter Olympics, the Lillehammer Olympic Organizing Committee distributed 100,000 "smile boeyles," or "smiling hoops" in an attempt to encourage citizens to look happy. The hoops consisted of rubber bands with plastic hooks that wrap behind one's head and attach at the corners of the mouth, thus forcing a smile.

A DUTCH POTATO PROCESSING COMPANY in Avebe received a government grant to see if starch made from potatoes can replace silicon in breast implants.

CHIP ALTHOLZ AND BARRY FALDNER OF Chicago invented the Timisis LifeClock. The $99.95 device, shaped like a 3-D triangle, allows you to program in your age and gender and then counts down the average number of hours, minutes and seconds remaining in your life span. The program assumes that men will live until the age of 75 years and women till the age of 80. Each minute the clock also flashes one of 150 motivational messages. Said Faldner, "We're born, they wind us up and say, 'Go and see what you can make of your life.' It's all about optimism."

OFFICIALS AT A NAPALM FACTORY IN Shostka, Ukraine, seeking the perfect product for the post–cold war world, developed "tourist matches," three-inch napalm-tipped matches advertised as ideal for campers, utility workers and homemakers. The matches light when wet and stay lit for at least a minute. The fire is so intense, however, that in one experiment one match burned through a half-inch glass ashtray, the quarter-inch-thick wooden table the ashtray sat on and proceeded to set fire to the rug below. Fumes from a single match set off smoke detectors 50 feet away. The matches can't be extinguished by blowing on them or by water. Stepping on a glowing napalm match only fractures it into numerous little pieces which continue to glow. The match box features a warning pictograph of a half-burned naked man and a burned field of tree stumps. A box of 45 sells for 25 cents.

TIMEX AWARDED $15,000 TO PETER
Doughty, a British civil servant who invented a machine that precisely measures women's busts. According to *The Guardian* newspaper, Doughty got the idea from his brother, who suggested using a box with light-emitting diodes and sensors to measure children's feet, not just length and width, but also height. Doughty's wife asked if the device might measure bosoms since she had read that seven out of 10 women had ill-fitting bras.

Give Us That
New-Time Religion

AT THE FIRST INTERNATIONAL WORKSHOP on Bad Breath, held in Tel Aviv, Shlomo Goren, a former chief rabbi of Israel, declared that bad breath is a legitimate reason for divorce. He said that several couples had been granted divorces in recent years after citing halitosis.

THE ROMAN CATHOLIC CHURCH GAVE ITS blessing to merchandising the pope's 1993 visit to the United States. More than 100 church-sanctioned items were available, including T-shirts, fanny packs and the Pope-Scope, which allows the viewer to see over the heads of those standing in front. To oversee the licensing arrangements, the church hired Famous Artists Merchandising Exchange, which has represented the Rolling Stones, Paul McCartney, Paul Simon, the Toronto Blue Jays and the University of Notre Dame. John C. Lemke, president of the Dayton, Ohio, company, predicted that sales of licensed products would amount to at least $6.5 million and could defray as much as 20 percent of the expenses of the pope's visit.

FOUR FAMILIES IN BURLINGTON COUNTY,
New Jersey, sued the Catholic Church, because it failed to remove a priest whom they accused of sexually abusing their children three years earlier. Claiming damages for emotional distress, the suit charges that by keeping the priest, the church caused them to lose their faith, lowering their chances of going to heaven.

IN JERUSALEM, RABBI YOSEF GINSBERG
authorized Israelis waiting in line to use force if necessary to prevent people from cutting in front of them.

THE SOUTHERN BAPTIST CONVENTION
identified people in Alabama who are going to hell.
Estimating that 46.1 percent of Alabama residents are
potentially doomed to going to hell when they die, the
church conducted a county-by-county study of the
state and determined that there were 1.86 million "un-
saved" souls. By taking each county's population and
subtracting church memberships in each county, then
applying a "secret formula," the Baptist researchers
estimated how many people from different denominations and faiths were bound for glory.

The group estimated the fate of believers in different faiths on the basis of how closely the beliefs of
each faith matched Baptist doctrine. Factored into the
equation was the assumption that Jews, Hindus, Bud-
dhists and believers in other non-Christian religions
were automatically bound for hell. The Southern Baptist Convention explained that the survey's purpose
was to provide a guide for determining where to build
new churches.

IN ENGLAND, THE REVEREND DEREK
Sawyer, complaining that worshipers weren't putting
enough money into the collection plate at St. Aldate's
Church in Gloucester, suggested that "perhaps the
only way forward is to say you can only belong to a
church if you pay a subscription." A year earlier, Sawyer suggested that worshipers bring their own bread

and wine to church for communion in order to further cut costs.

THE 1,200 RESIDENTS OF TWO BOMBAY apartment buildings threw their television sets out the window to protest violence and sex on Indian TV. According to the *Pioneer* newspaper, the action began when Safira Ali Mohammad and her family disconnected their set, carried it to the window of their highrise apartment and hurled it down. Minutes later, neighbors who heard the crash also pushed their sets out of the window. Most of them are Muslims who were constantly told at prayer meetings that TV programs corrupt youngsters.

WHEN THE CHURCH OF ENGLAND DIS-missed the Reverend Anthony Freeman, 48, after he publicly proclaimed that there is no God, 65 of his fellow clergy protested the firing. They said that Anglican authorities should be more tolerant of unorthodox views.

IN THE TOWN OF GUJRANWALA, PAKI-
stan, an angry mob doused a devout Muslim doctor
with kerosene and burned him to death after he was
accused of setting fire to the Koran, Islam's holy book.
The newspaper *Jang* reported that the doctor, Farooq
Sajjad, burned a page of the Koran after he accidentally knocked it from his wife's hands during an argument and it landed on the stove and burned.

IRAN'S INTERIOR MINISTRY ORDERED PEO-
ple to stop stabbing themselves in the head during
Muslim Shi'ite mourning rituals. "Wounding one's head
with daggers is not in Islamic tradition," spiritual
leader Ayatollah Ali Khamenei said. "We should not do
things that would make us appear as a superstitious
and illogical group in the eyes of Muslims and non-
Muslims of the world."

A MECHANICAL MEANS OF COLLECTING
sperm for medical use was touted as a moral alterna-
tive to masturbation by an article published by Catholic University of the Sacred Heart in Rome, which is
under the direction of Italian bishops. Masturbation is
the most common way to gather sperm for laboratory

tests related to impotence and genetic diseases, but the Catholic Church teaches that masturbation is immoral. The article described the use of a vibrating machine that attaches to a testicle, concluding from a survey of 17 men who used the machine that "several components that constitute the masturbation act would seem to be absent" such as "direct stimulation of the genital organ" and any "erotic feelings."

THE CATHOLIC MAGAZINE *FAMIGLIA CRIStiana* published an editorial urging priests with mobile telephones not to take them to the confessional or at least remember to switch them off while administering the sacrament. The editorial followed a complaint from a reader who insisted that her confession was made even more stressful by the phone ringing.

4.

DUMB AS CHARGED

Curses,
Foiled Again

KIDNAPPERS WHO ABDUCTED GILDO DOS Santos near his factory in a suburb of São Paulo, Brazil, demanded $690,000, but Santos escaped. The next day, Santos got a phone call asking for $11,500 to defray the cost of the abduction. After negotiating a discount of 50 percent, Santos called police, who were waiting when Luiz Carlos Valerio showed up to collect payment.

TWO ARMED MEN WHO CONFRONTED THE night clerk at the AmeriSuites Hotel in Little Rock, Arkansas, apparently didn't case the place first or they would have discovered the hotel was serving as a temporary dormitory for the heavily armed Secret Service contingent guarding President-elect Bill Clinton and Vice President-elect Al Gore. An agent who saw the holdup chased the gunmen in a van, joined by other agents, who shot two of the three men in the getaway car. "Didn't they think anything was unusual when they saw the parking lot?" one agent wondered, noting that the hotel parking lot was crowded with Jeep Cherokees, Chryslers and unmarked vans, all with District of Columbia license plates and emergency lights in their grillework.

OFFICIALS AT OHIO'S PICKAWAY CORREC-

tional Institute stopped two cars that drove into a restricted area. A check of their license plates revealed both cars were stolen. Authorities apprehended the drivers, Jessi N. Kase, 20, and James J. Kalb, 23, and two teenage girls accompanying them who turned out to be runaways. According to the highway patrol, the men had driven onto the correctional center grounds to show the girls where they had once served time.

THREE CHINESE SMUGGLERS WERE AR-

rested in the Russian Far East for trying to enter the country with 1,078,000 rubles in bank notes taped to their bodies. The notes, in denominations of 1,000 rubles, were hidden under their clothes, according to *Moskovsky Komsomolets*, which reported customs officers were alerted by the rustling sound of paper as the smugglers walked past.

AFTER EDILBER GUIMARAES, 19, BROKE
into a glue factory in Belo Horizonte, Brazil, he began sniffing the glue he was stealing. Overcome by the fumes, he collapsed, upsetting a tank of glue. When he came to, he found himself stuck to the floor, unable to tear himself free. He lay there for 36 hours, *Globo* TV reported, before firefighters managed to cut him loose.

SIX TEENAGERS IN NEW HOLLAND, PENN-
sylvania, beat and robbed a group of Amish, thinking they were Old Order Amish and Groffdale Conference Mennonites, two old sects that traditionally do not contact police when they are crime victims. Instead, the victims were Plain Sect Amish, who do call police—and did. The youths, who beat their victims with brooms and hit them with rocks and corn, were arrested and charged.

IN LONDON, A 35-YEAR-OLD DIVORCED
mother of three arrested after a shoplifting spree defended herself by telling the court that getting arrested
was the only way she could achieve an orgasm. She
claimed that the sirens and flashing blue lights of police cars really turned her on. The prosecution dis-
missed her defense as "a load of rubbish." The court
agreed and fined her $300.

FIREFIGHTERS WHO ENTERED AN ABAN-
doned house in West Palm Beach, Florida, after dous-
ing a blaze found the body of the asphyxiated arsonist,
still clutching a matchbook. Investigators said that William Grace, 33, probably spilled flammable liquid on
himself as he spread it around the house, then when
he lit the fire and the liquid on him blew up, he pan-
icked and ran blindly until he hit his head.

IN ALBUQUERQUE, NEW MEXICO, JAMES
Chavez, 41, and Jimmy Garcia, 31, bought cocaine with
$10 from Chavez and $8 from Garcia. When the men
were unable to figure out how to split the drug, they
began fighting, according to police, and stabbed each
other to death.

TWO BURGLARS ENTERED A CHEMICAL
fertilizer business in Martin, Ohio, by throwing a chunk
of concrete through the window. After trashing the offices, they tried to open the safe by using a front-end
loader to smash it against the side of a building. It
crashed through the wall but didn't open. Next they
smashed it against the side of a utility trailer. Still unsuccessful, they placed the four-foot-high, 1,000-pound,
concrete-lined strongbox on nearby railroad tracks in
the path of a freight train. "You name it, they did it,"
Sheriff Craig Emahiser said, explaining that the train
pushed the safe about a mile down the tracks, far from
the burglars, before the door popped open. By then,
the frustrated safecrackers had fled.

RAYMOND CUTHBERT ENTERED A DRUG
store in Vernon, British Columbia, and announced that
he and his partner would be back in half an hour to
rob the place. Employees called the Royal Canadian
Mounted Police, who arrested Cuthbert and Robert
Phimister when they returned as promised.

CLAIMING TO HAVE A SHOTGUN UNDER
his long coat, Sasuualei Faamausili Jr., 26, robbed a
video store in Daly City, California. As he left, he spot-

ted Arthur Azucena, 44, pulled the shotgun from under his long coat, aimed it at Azucena and demanded money. According to police, when Azucena saw the shotgun was just two crib legs wrapped together in plastic, he pulled a real pistol and shot Faamausili dead.

IN MIAMI, MEXICAN ZOO OFFICIAL VICTOR Bernal, 57, was convicted of violating U.S. endangered species laws for trying to pay $92,500 for a gorilla that turned out to be a U.S. Fish and Wildlife Service agent wearing a gorilla suit. In the sting operation, Bernal fell for the deception and asked for a plane and a pilot to fly him and the gorilla back to Mexico. When agents arrested him, Bernal still thought the gorilla in a crate was real, especially when the agent got out of the crate. "We kept telling him, 'We're police! We're po- lice!' " said Special Agent Monty Halcomb, who posed as the plane's pilot. "But even after the agent took the hood off, he couldn't believe a gorilla wasn't coming after him."

RICHARD C. JORDAN, 22, WAS CHARGED with abducting a Lakewood, Colorado, woman, then driving to the nearest ATM to withdraw money. "I told him I didn't have an ATM card because I don't like machines, but that I could go to King Soopers [super-market] to cash a check," the victim said.

The suspect agreed and stayed in the car while the woman went into the store, where she alerted the manager. To buy time while waiting for the police, the victim went back to her car and told the suspect she needed her driver's license to cash a check. The suspect was still waiting when police arrived.

WHEN SAN ANTONIO, TEXAS, POLICE caught Terry Allen, 34, removing burglar bars from the window of a beauty salon, they charged him with attempted burglary. He insisted that he was guilty only of theft since he wasn't trying to break into the beauty salon, merely trying to steal the burglar bars to put on his own windows to protect himself from burglars.

IN DENVER, A MAN WIELDING A KNIFE tried to hold up the gift shop at the Stapleton Plaza Hotel, but was foiled when he couldn't operate the cash register.

PAUL BRENNAN III, 24, PERSUADED PO-
lice in New Britain, Connecticut, to let him set up a
can next to a picture of a rescue boat at the police
station to raise money for state lifeguards. About 50
officers donated $59 before officials learned that Bren-
nan had been arrested 13 times for fraud and ordered
by the state to stop soliciting donations. Police arrested him when he stopped by the station to collect
the money.

WHEN SHERIFF'S DEPUTIES IN CHARLES
City County, Virginia, stopped a van driven by Alfred
E. Acree to arrest him for drug dealing, Acree jumped
out and ran into the dense woods. Even though it was
nighttime, deputies were able to follow Acree because
he was wearing L.A. Gear battery-operated sneakers,
which flash when the heel is pressed. "Every time he
took a step, we knew exactly where he was," Investigator Anthony Anderson said.

POLICE IN ROCHESTER, NEW YORK, AR-
rested Roland James, 34, whom they suspected of robbing the same bank three times within 24 hours, after

they found him outside the bank waiting for it to open so he could rob it again.

AFTER LEAVING A FORT LAUDERDALE, Florida, court hearing where they were charged with stealing 25 cars, two boys, aged 14 and 15, stole another car because neither had enough money for the bus fare home.

A GROUP OF RUSSIAN COUNTERFEITERS produced a near-perfect run of bogus 50,000-ruble bank notes. Once they went into general circulation officials agreed that it was an excellent job and appeared to be genuine currency. Their only error was misspelling "Russia."

JORGE RODRIGUEZ, 22, SPOKE NO ENGlish and had no lawyer when he appeared in a Kenosha, Wisconsin, court on charges of hitting a parked car and drunk driving. However, he was confident in his chances when he approached the judge and handed over a card reading GET OUT OF JAIL FREE. Eight thousand of the cards had been printed and distributed by a local candidate for sheriff in that year's election. "Clearly the defendant had the impression it was legitimate and was going to play that trump card," said the assistant city attorney. Instead, the judge suspended his license and fined him $1,107.

WHEN NEW YORK CITY POLICE STOPPED James Wright, 25, for driving the wrong way on a one-way street, he offered them a $40 bribe to forget about it. When they declined, he upped the offer to an AK-47 assault rifle, a .45-caliber semiautomatic handgun, a .32-caliber revolver and $300 in cash. They promptly arrrested him.

FEARING THAT POLICE WOULD NOTICE HIS distinctive clothing, suspected bank robber Travion Davis, 19, stopped in a south Los Angeles alley and disrobed. Sheriff's deputies spotted the naked man and chased him down the alley and over some fences before arresting him and taking his two shopping bags filled with $15,000.

WHEN STATE POLICE IN OGDENSBURG, New York, caught William J. Hess, 39, burglarizing a greenhouse, he was wearing nothing. He explained that he was naked so that anyone who saw him in the greenhouse couldn't identify him by describing his clothing.

POLICE IN MONTGOMERY COUNTY, MARYland, arrested 32-year-old Norman Alafriz Toro, and charged him with possession of $500,000 in counterfeit $100 bills. The fake money was spearmint-colored and apparently had been produced on a copying machine.

FOUR WOMEN ATTACKED ANOTHER woman with a chemical spray after she reportedly beat them to a parking space at a shopping mall in Glendale, California. Police searching the parking lot for the women found them arguing because they had locked the keys in the car. After finding the chemical spray and charging the women with assault, officers helped open their car—and found shoplifted clothing on the backseat.

Not-So-Great
Escapes and
Getaways

IN FRANCE, THREE INMATES BROKE OUT
of a new prison near Aix-en-Provence by climbing lad-
ders left behind by workers who were erecting wires
intended to deter helicopter-aided escapes from prison
yards.

MARK RYAN OF LYNN, MASSACHUSETTS,
may have fooled bank tellers, customers, passersby
and a cab driver, but he couldn't fool the police. After
donning a disguise and robbing the Equitable Cooper-
ative Bank of $4,466, Ryan walked outside, wearing his

mask, and hailed a taxi. He was still masked when a police officer spotted him in the cab and arrested him.

AFTER ROBBING A BANK IN ROUEN, France, Jules Duprer leapt into a car and shouted to the driver, "Get away quick before the cops come." It was a police car.

DURING A MASS BREAKOUT BY 62 PRIS-oners from a police detention center in São Paulo, Brazil, one of the escapees, convicted robber Daniel Salustiano da Costa, 29, was running from the jail when he heard an ambulance siren. He turned to look for it and ran headlong into a lamppost, killing himself.

WHEN A POLICE VAN STOPPED AT AN IN-tersection in Adelaide, Australia, two prisoners handcuffed together broke out and tried to run away. They were stopped when they tried to run on either side of a utility pole, according to police spokesperson Ken

Gunn, who explained, "It was just like in the movies, the feet went up in the air."

......

A MAN WHO ROBBED A NEW YORK CITY bank was making his getaway when he ran into 25 housing police officers on a training exercise. Raymond Wilson, 20, immediately changed direction, just as the officers heard the suspect's description broadcast on their radios and gave chase. The suspect fled through the front door of a building, but it turned out to be the housing police precinct station house, where he was arrested with $5,000 on him.

......

POLICE IN LA CROSSE, WISCONSIN, COULD only charge Ronald Gollnick, 47, with attempted bank robbery, even though the teller handed over $800 after he threatened to shoot her. When Gollnick left the bank, he forgot to take the money with him.

......

AFTER LEADING POLICE IN FREMONT, CALifornia, on a chase, during which he ran 15 red lights and sideswiped several cars, Michael Anthony Dorsey was finally halted when he slammed his 1980 Corvette into the city jail. "He didn't have too far to go from there," said police Cpt. Mike Lanam. "It was like a drive-up window."

IN TAMPA, FLORIDA, ROBBERY SUSPECT Kenneth Carlton Bamber, 35, led police on a 118-mile chase, during which he rarely exceeded the speed limit and obeyed all traffic laws. According to Hillsborough County sheriff's spokesperson Jack Espinosa, deputies, who didn't want to cause an accident, calmly pursued Bamber for an hour and 37 minutes until one annoyed deputy drew alongside him and shouted, "All right, that's enough, now pull over!"

ARKANSAS INMATES RANDALL ROWLAND, 28, and Frank Wade, 31, broke out of the Saline County jail in November, then stole a milk truck. They failed to close the rear doors, however, letting cartons of milk spill out of the back, according to Sheriff Judy Pridgen, who said, "After they got ahold of the milk truck, we were just minutes behind them and following the trail of milk cartons they were leaving."

IN LANCASTER, CALIFORNIA, STEVEN BRI-
gida, 25, escaped from a minimum-security prison by
hiding in a trash bin, but the bin was collected by a
truck that crushes garbage into a bale about one-fifth
the size of the original load. Brigida was discovered at
a landfill by the operator of a bladed tractor used to
break up garbage bales. "He alerted us that he was a
prisoner," Mike Muller, general manager of Waste Management of Lancaster, said. "I think his escape plan
was gone by then."

AFTER SERVING 89 DAYS OF A 90-DAY
sentence in prison for a disorderly conduct charge, a
34-year-old Newport, Rhode Island, man escaped. If re-
captured, he would face the possibility of 20 years in
prison, prison spokesperson Joseph DiNitto said, adding, "For the life of me I don't know what possessed
him to leave with only one day of his sentence left to
serve."

Latter-Day
Willie Suttons

A GUNMAN IN COLUMBIA, TENNESSEE, announced a bank robbery, but the bank had closed eight months earlier. "He walked in here and said, 'Give me your money,' and I laughed," said Lea Ables, who works for the insurance company that moved into the office. "I didn't think he was serious at first. He then sort of looked funny and asked, 'This ain't a bank anymore?'"

TWO GUNMEN WEARING SKI MASKS burst into the Old Colony Credit Bureau in Plymouth, Massachusetts, ordered the owner and three other workers to lie on the floor, then ransacked the office, taking a small amount of cash and some jewelry. Police were baffled why the robbers would target Old Colony, which compiles credit reports and keeps little cash on hand, although some officials speculated that the holdup was a botched bank robbery, with the robbers mistaking the credit bureau for a credit union.

IN ARLINGTON, VIRGINIA, A MAN PRE-sented a check for $1,450 to a bank teller, who told him to wait for approval and took the check to Assistant Vice President Melinda Babson. She knew the woman whose check it was but didn't recognize the signature, so she called her. The woman said she had not written the check, which Babson then copied and faxed to her.

The whole time, the unsuspecting suspect waited calmly, sipping a cup of coffee, according to Senior Vice President Andrew Flott, who noted after police arrived and arrested the man, "He was a knucklehead for not leaving." Even if he had left, the teller had his driver's license, which he had given her for identification with the check.

IN SAN DIEGO, A 75-YEAR-OLD MAN WAS arrested for stealing $70 from a bank. The man, who sat in a motorized wheelchair, had threatened to blow up the bank with his nitroglycerin heart pills.

BANK ROBBERS IN COOPERVILLE, OHIO,

drilled through the door of a bank safe, came upon a brick wall, drilled through that and discovered that they had ended up on the street outside the bank.

A 42-YEAR-OLD COLUMBUS, OHIO, MAN

pleaded guilty to a bank robbery and was sentenced to five years probation. He was caught when, due to his curiosity, he hung around in the crowd of onlookers who had gathered outside the bank in the wake of his robbery. A bank employee noticed him in the crowd and pointed him out to police.

A NORFOLK, VIRGINIA, MAN SUSPECTED

of two bank robberies was easily identified from bank security camera photos despite his disguise. He attempted to obscure his appearance by using only three small adhesive bandages. Two were placed above his eyebrows and the third across his nose.

POLICE IN VIRGINIA BEACH, VIRGINIA, charged Charles Robertson, 19, with robbing a bank when he bungled his way into their hands. After handing the teller a holdup note, Robertson started to flee but stopped when he realized that he had forgot his note. He dashed back and grabbed the note, but this time he left the keys to his getaway car—a fact he didn't discover until he reached the vehicle. He managed to elude police, but when he got home he told his roommate, whose car he had borrowed, that it had been stolen. She reported the car missing, and about 20 minutes later Officer Mike Koch spotted it a block from the bank. Playing a hunch, Koch got the keys the robbery suspect had left behind. When they fit the car that had been reported stolen, detectives went to the address the owner had given and found Robertson.

POLICE IN DES MOINES ARRESTED RON- ald Albert Siedelman, 56, as he stood outside a downtown bank. Siedelman had walked into the bank and presented a long rambling note demanding $19 trillion. While bank employees tried to decipher the barely legible and confusing note, Siedelman stepped outside to smoke a cigarette because, according to police, he didn't want to violate the bank's no-smoking policy.

POLICE IN STRATFORD, CONNECTICUT, AR-
rested Lee W. Womble, 28, for robbing a bank after he
handed the teller a withdrawal slip with "the money"
scribbled on it, along with his name. "He wrote his
name on it twice," detective Lt. Thomas Roadia explained. "Once on top of the other."

Why They
Call It Dope

IN ARLINGTON, VIRGINIA, DONALD FLOOD,
40, was sentenced to prison for bigamy after he married three women within 45 days. He blamed his wedding spree on drugs. When he realized he had three
wives, Flood said, "I didn't care. I wanted to love
someone."

FACING STOLEN PROPERTY, DANGEROUS
driving and probation violation charges, Lincoln
MacKenzie, 20, appeared in court in Brantford, Ontario, carrying a gym bag that turned out to contain 18
bags of marijuana. "How stupid can you get?" Provin-

cial Court Judge M. J. Perozak asked after MacKenzie pleaded guilty to old and new charges.

....

IN CALIFORNIA, A SMALL PLANE LANDED at night without landing lights at Castle Air Force Base while Air Force stratotankers were practicing landings and takeoffs. After air traffic controllers took quick action to alert the tanker crews and avoid a collision, Merced County sheriff's deputies searched the plane and found two pounds of methamphetamines and $1,300 in cash. They arrested pilot Edward Velez, 25, and passenger José Gonzalez, 33, who told officers that they believed they were landing at a small airport 20 miles to the north.

....

POLICE IN CORAM, NEW YORK, REPORTED that a man flagged down an unmarked police car and offered two detectives crack cocaine to drive him home. According to police spokesperson Mark Ryan, the detectives were just returning from a drug bust and were wearing blue jackets identifying them as SUFFOLK COUNTY POLICE in big white letters.

BROTHERS MICHAEL MURPHY JR., 19,
and Eric Murphy, 16, drove to a state police barracks
in Southbury, Connecticut, to deliver medication to
their father, who was being held on larceny charges.
They parked in a spot marked "Reserved for Duty Ser-
geant," causing the dispatcher to run a computer
check, which showed the car was reported stolen.
When troopers took the youths into custody, one of
them was carrying a pipe packed with marijuana. A
search of the car's glove compartment yielded 18 bags
of marijuana, packaged for street sale, and a weapon.

POLICE IN RICHMOND, VIRGINIA, WERE LED
to Collin H. Hudson III, 23, by a telephone number on
business cards advertising crack cocaine. One card announced, "Head Crack! Head Crack! Weight Is Good
So True Pipers Will Be Back!" Prices were listed at
between $20 and $240. Another card read "Cook 'Em
Up!" and gave the hours of drug availability. It said that
the dealer would be "walking from corner to corner
with boom box." When police raided Hudson's home
they found one pound of cocaine and 1,000 business
cards.

UNDERCOVER POLICE POSING AS DRUG
dealers in Huntington Beach, California, arrested 20
men and women in an alley over the course of a night
as they purchased what they believed to be cocaine.
"I'll tell you how bright these people are," said police
Lieut. Patrick Gildea. "We actually had people coming
up and getting in line [to buy drugs] when we had people [under arrest and handcuffed] on the ground." In
one case a woman walked up to a uniformed officer
wearing a jacket with the word POLICE spelled out in
eight-inch letters and asked if she could buy cocaine
from him.

DISTRICT OF COLUMBIA ETHICS CHIEF
Robert Lane pleaded guilty to driving his government-
issue car to buy $60 worth of crack cocaine from a
street-corner drug dealer. Lane quit his $82,000-a-year
job overseeing financial and ethical conduct of city officials after he was put on probation.

POLICE IN THE PERSIAN GULF CITY OF DU-
bai reported arresting a number of youths who get in-
toxicated by smoking ants or sniffing the fumes ants
emit when they're crushed, according to the *Gulf*

News. Noting that a small packet of ants sells for up to $135 in Abu Dhabi, authorities explained that teenagers are turning to ants because they can't afford other drugs or think they won't be prosecuted.

BRITISH CUSTOMS AGENTS ARRESTED

Robert Ventham, 22, when he returned from buying drugs in Gibraltar, despite his attempt to fool them as to the real purpose of his trip by carrying a set of golf clubs. The ruse only alerted the agents because Gibraltar has no golf courses.

You Eeeddiiottt!

IN SOUTH KOREA, SEOUL POLICE
charged Park Han-sang with murdering his parents. "I
decided to kill them as I was badly scolded for spending too much money," he was quoted as saying. "I got
the idea of inheriting their property if they died."

FACING SHOPLIFTING CHARGES IN PIE-
termaritzburg, South Africa, Michael Dladla, 22, said at
a court hearing that he took candy because he wanted
to go to jail like Nelson Mandela and write a book
about the experience. He asked for life imprisonment.
After spending several days in jail, Dladla agreed at a
second hearing to be released with a warning.

TWO MEN AND A WOMAN IN SAN DIEGO,
frustrated after coming up empty-handed when they
tried to rob a penniless, homeless man named Richard
at about 4 A.M., started beating the man. They told him
they would stop if he could get them some money
somewhere. He suggested a friend, so they drove him
to the friend's house. He went inside but returned to
say that his friends had no money (and no phone he
could use to call police). He suggested other friends
living nearby. The would-be robbers drove Richard to
the second house, but again, no cash and no phone.
At a third house, Richard went in, then his friend Ron
Williams walked outside to verify his story. Wearing
only a bathrobe, he approached the car and peered
inside. "Oh, I thought you were someone else," he
apologized, then went back in and called the police,
who found Thomas Bray, Todd Kirby and Lori Stanton
still waiting in the car. Police spokesperson Bill Rob-
inson noted, "They were no Einsteins."

GHANAIAN POLICE OFFICER MUSTAPHA
Garbah told a court in Accra that he had stopped a
Ford Escort for speeding. "I thought the family in the
car were all very ugly," he explained. "Then I saw that
the fourteen passengers were all pregnant goats in
T-shirts." Driver John Ofosu admitted stealing the animals from villages in the Ashanti region.

MICHAEL WRIGHTMAN, 30, PLEADED guilty in Toronto to beating David Marlatt to death. He explained that he attacked the victim during an argument over which one of them had the longer criminal record.

POLICE IN BROOKSVILLE, FLORIDA, ACcused Anne Bloxsom, 26, of slashing her boss's throat and robbing an office safe to pay for her four-year-old daughter to participate in a beauty pageant.

MICHAEL WRIGHT AND STEVEN BEAN, both 18, stole $400 from the Chelmsford, Massachusetts, gas station where they worked, then shot each other in the shoulder to make it look as if they were victims of a holdup. The two confessed while being questioned in the hospital, according to police Lieut. Francis Roark, who noted they "are lucky they didn't kill each other."

POLICE IN SOUTH DEERFIELD, MASSA-chusetts, arrested James Feeley, 25, and Luis Cortez, 25, for walking into a police station and trying to attack the officer on duty. Officer Robert Wagner said that when he stopped the men from entering a dispatch area, Feeley pulled a nightstick and shouted, "Shoot me," then continued forward. Wagner disarmed Feeley, and fellow officers who came to his aid took both men into custody. Feeley, who lives just a few hundred yards from the police station, explained he went there "to clean house."

IN PHILADELPHIA, DAVID JOHNSON, 29, RE-ported to municipal court for a hearing on charges that he stole a 1989 Cutlass Ciera. Arresting officers Christopher Foley and John Wolk testified against him. Ten minutes after the hearing, the officers noticed a 1986 Buick Regal make an illegal U-turn and pulled up beside it. Johnson was driving the car, which had been reported stolen.

IN FREDERICK, MARYLAND, CARMEN
Friedewald-Hill, 26, shot boyfriend Ryan Gesner to death during an argument over which one of them loved the other more.

STEPHANIE A. CARTER, 20, OF TAKOMA

Park, Maryland, was arrested when she phoned a cab company to complain that she was charged too much for a ride to a house that authorities said she intended to rob. Seeking a suspect who took a county worker's purse, which contained her house keys, then showed up at the worker's house in a cab but left when a dog inside the house barked, Sgt. Robert Keefer of the Montgomery County sheriff's department began calling local taxi companies. One dispatcher said he had a woman on the other line complaining that the fare to the address Keefer gave was too much. At Keefer's request, the dispatcher got Carter's name and address.

IN WOODBRIDGE, NEW JERSEY, THOMAS

Lynch, 64, who was upset with a delay in selling his house, stabbed real estate agent Nancy McManus, 46, to death. He set the house on fire to hide the crime but accidentally killed himself, investigators said, noting that Lynch left a trail of gasoline behind him going down the stairs. "When he lit a match," Middlesex County Prosecutor Robert Gluck explained, "the gasoline blew up in his face and apparently incapacitated him."

HAMILTON COUNTY, INDIANA, SHERIFF'S
detectives charged Charles D. Carey with theft for accepting a $50 gift certificate for second place in a charity golf tournament. Acting on a tip, they had followed Carey during his round at Hanging Tree Golf Club and said he shaved at least 13 strokes from his score. Curiously, each golfer had paid a $75 entry fee, but authorities said Carey apparently was expecting a much higher payoff, based on prizes awarded at previous charity tournaments where he is suspected of cheating.

AFTER REPRESENTING HIMSELF IN COURT
and twice winning acquittals on charges of writing worthless checks and assault, Reinero Torres Jr., 53, of Sebring, Florida, lost a third case. He was convicted of theft for having stolen law books from the courthouse library to prepare his defense for the first two cases.

IN AURORA, COLORADO, RONNELL ROPER,
21, was wounded in the head, torso, arms and legs after he and an accomplice broke into a gun show, and well-armed security guards opened fire.

IN AUBURN, NEW YORK, MARK D. COL-
lins, 34, pleaded guilty to stealing money that never
existed. Collins, a $12,000-a-year ticket seller at a state
off-track betting parlor, used his computer to place
bets for himself without putting up any cash. He bet
$60 on the first race but lost. He continued betting on
the favorites and losing, then increasing the next bet
to cover his losses. By the tenth race, his bet was
$28,500. Finally, his horse won. Unfortunately, the
odds were so low that the payoff still left him $38,105
short of the $80,280 he had bet, and he was arrested.

 , After Collins received five years probation, the In-
ternal Revenue Service billed him for taxes on the entire amount because that was the sum embezzled. The
IRS did credit him for the $42,175 in winning tickets
he surrendered, but said he couldn't deduct the
$38,105 as gambling losses against his winnings since
he never received any actual money. An appeals court
affirmed that Collins owed the IRS $9,376 on the non-
money he lost.

IN SAN FRANCISCO, LOVERS JOANN TRE-
thewey, 20, and John David Martin, 26, plotted to kill
Martin's wife Rebecca, 32, by having Trethewey open
fire on her and a crowd of bystanders in a movie parking lot and to make it look like a random attack by a
gang or a maniac. But all 20 bullets fired by the HK-94
assault weapon hit Rebecca's Nissan Pathfinder, in-

cluding four that wounded but did not kill her. Suspicious that a gang would single her out for such an assault, investigators discovered other flaws in the scheme. For example, Martin and Trethewey had purchased a $500,000 insurance policy on his wife just before the attack. Afterward, they threw the gun into the water at high tide, leaving it exposed at low tide. "It's really the most detective storybook type of case I've ever been confronted with," Deputy District Attorney Mary Ann O'Malley said.

IN BIRMINGHAM, ALABAMA, ALEX THO-

mas, 21, was indicted for using other people's credit cards to order more than $5,000 worth of pizzas at a restaurant during three months last year. He got the credit card numbers from guests at a hotel where he worked as a desk clerk, according to Assistant U.S. Attorney Mike Whisonant. "I don't know exactly how many pizzas we're talking about, but he went to the restaurant 73 times and ordered four to six pizzas each time," Whisonant said, adding that Thomas, who weighs 350 pounds, gave some of the pizzas to friends, "but we believe he ate a lot of them himself."

ATTORNEY EARL BRODY, REPRESENTING

defendant Henry Keith Watson in the Reginald Denny beating trial stemming from the Los Angeles riot, told the jury that videotaped scenes in which Watson stepped on trucker Denny's neck as he lay in the street were being misinterpreted. Brody explained that Watson "gingerly" placed his foot on Denny's neck in an attempt "to protect Mr. Denny from further assault."

ATTORNEY ATIQ AHMED, ONE OF THE lawyers defending the four Islamic fundamentalist defendants accused in the World Trade Center bombing, objected to government prosecutors' use of the word *bomb*. Ahmed said that he didn't believe that the government could prove that there was a bomb involved.

JOHN ASONIUS, 41, BARRED FROM TAPING his trial in Stockholm, Sweden, used his tape recorder to beat up his two court-appointed defense attorneys. Guards overpowered Asonius and dragged him from the courtroom as the court-appointed attorneys wiped blood from their foreheads. The proceedings resumed hours later, with the attorneys sitting farther away from their client.

POLICE IN FORT PIERCE, FLORIDA, charged Richard Dorsey, 19, with robbing a grave when they found bones in the trunk of his car. Dorsey explained that he needed the bones to measure for a coffin he was building that he planned to use for Halloween, but when he went to return the bones a few days later, the grave had been filled in.

POLICE IN BAKERSFIELD, CALIFORNIA, chased two suspects in a liquor store robbery 25 miles to Lamont, where one of the men pulled a gun. Before the suspect could fire, officers shot him in the arm and leg. The wounded man's weapon turned out to be a toy pistol.

Fifth-Amendment Follies

DAVID LEE MCCUMSEY JR., 18, WAS charged with stealing two handguns and a watch from a hardware store in Homosassa Springs, Florida. Employees noticed the items missing after the teen had applied for a job, then left in a hurry, leaving behind his completed job application. Store manager Joe Clark observed, "It was about the dumbest thing I have ever seen."

A JURY TOOK ONLY 80 MINUTES TO CONvict Lee S. Francis of shooting his former girlfriend in Kansas City, Missouri, despite his statements denying the crime. In fact, his denial helped convict him. He insisted to police that he didn't shoot the victim with a small .25-caliber semiautomatic pistol while running alongside her car, although the police hadn't disclosed any information about how the 18-year-old woman died or the gun used to kill her.

HARTFORD, CONNECTICUT, POLICE OFFICER

Joao Q. Nunes, 36, admitted trying to rob a bank after investigators found his business card in a briefcase that he reportedly told bank employees contained a bomb.

POLICE IN BRAINTREE, MASSACHUSETTS,

charged Robert C. Mercon, 19, with two bank robberies after matching the handwriting on the two holdup notes to that of a note found in Mercon's pocket after he was picked up on shoplifting charges. In all three notes, the writer had switched the *i* and the *e* in *thief*.

DALE WOOD, 25, CHARGED IN THE SHOT-

gun murder of a banker, asked a Maine court to suppress his confession, explaining that he was im-

properly pressured by police who took advantage of
his addiction to cigarettes. Wood said that during ques-
tioning at the nonsmoking jail, detectives gave him the
cigarettes he craved and he confessed.

POLICE IN MARSHALL, MINNESOTA, AR-
rested Scott Timothy Root, 31, for stealing a car after
they recovered it and found a copy of his job résumé
under one of the seats.

MICHAEL KOJIMA, 50, AGREED TO PLEAD
no contest to charges of failing to pay child support
after he was apprehended in Salt Lake City following
a five-month search. Describing Kojima as one of Los
Angeles County's biggest "deadbeat dads," who owed
more than $100,000, prosecutors said that while failing
to support his family, Kojima donated $500,000 at a
Republican fund-raiser. Authorities issued a warrant
for his arrest after they spotted him in news photos
from the April 28, 1992 dinner, sitting at President
Bush's table.

PAVLOS BATSIOS, 29, ONE OF GREECE'S most-wanted bank robbery suspects, was arrested at a police station when he showed up to report the theft of his sports car. Officers realized that the car fit the description of the getaway car used in at least two robberies. Batsios explained that he reported the theft because he feared police would question him if the stolen car was involved in an accident.

WHEN A JURY IN GASTONIA, NORTH CAR-olina, left the courtroom to deliberate the sexual assault case against a 52-year-old man, the defendant fled. "Apparently he was more impressed with the evidence than the jury was," Assistant District Attorney Mike Kromis said after the jury returned a verdict of not guilty.

IN FLINT, MICHIGAN, MICHAEL ALLEN, 26, appeared at his hearing on charges stemming from a house robbery wearing a green, double-breasted suit that he hoped would make a good impression on the judge. Instead, the victim announced, "He's wearing my suit." A check of the custom-made suit's label verified the claim.

A PRISON COUNSELOR IN COLUMBUS,
Ohio, stood in front of a criminal justice class and confessed to a 1979 murder. The man, who explained that
he believed the statute of limitations had run out, was
sentenced to 15 years to life.

So Sue Me

WHILE AWAITING TRANSFER FROM THE
Siloam Springs, Arkansas, jail to a state prison to serve
a 10-year sentence for drug trafficking, Ross Chadwell
was made a trusty. He took advantage of his privilege
by escaping. When he was captured two months later,
Chadwell filed a lawsuit against Benton County Sheriff
Andy Lee. Maintaining that Lee never should have
made him a trusty in the first place, Chadwell explained that the sheriff "violated this plaintiff's civil
rights when he permitted this plaintiff to escape."

A STUDENT AT NORWAY'S OSLO UNIVER-
sity filed a lawsuit against the school for preventing
him from taking examinations. The 39-year-old astro-

physics student, who began studying at the university in 1971, lives in a cave and wears torn and dirty clothes to class. "He has been banned from taking exams since 1981 because the university says his body and clothes smell so bad that he cannot sit in a room with other students," said his lawyer, Peter Graver, who explained that his client wanted a court to overrule the university's ban and award him $470,000.

A MORRIS COUNTY, NEW JERSEY, JURY awarded $500,000 to Jay Weiss, 29, who was severely injured when he tried to kill himself by setting fire to the mattress in his hotel room. He suffered massive burns on his legs and arms, and both legs had to be amputated. He sued a psychiatrist at a hospital he went to before the suicide attempt, complaining he was hearing voices in his head telling him to kill himself. Weiss contended that the psychiatrist was liable for his injuries because she failed to diagnose him as psychotic.

JERRY WALKER, 42, AN INMATE AT THE Southern New Mexico Correctional Facility, filed a lawsuit against the facility and the state Corrections Department, claiming the prison's medical staff failed to provide adequate treatment for persistent groin

pain. He said the pain ultimately drove him to remove
his own testicles.

A LOS ANGELES JURY AWARDED $300,000
to William Neuser, 49, whose penile implant didn't
work when it was supposed to. His lawsuit claimed
that the malfunction of the penile inflation device
made by American Medical Systems of Minnesota
caused a "devastating effect on his sex life."

A NEW YORK CITY JUDGE AWARDED $4.2
million to Hector Manuel Rivera, 43, who jumped in
front of a subway train and lost his legs. A social
worker at the state-run Manhattan Psychiatric Center
had handed subway tokens to Rivera, a mental patient,
and told him to move to a different hospital, according
to Rivera's attorney, Robert Tessler, who said his client
told him the devil told him to leap in front of the train.

FORMER UNIVERSITY OF IDAHO STUDENT
Jason Wilkins, who crashed through a third-story dormitory window while mooning friends on the ground,

filed a tort claim against the state for $940,000. Wilkins climbed on top of a three-foot-high heater in front of a plate-glass window, dropped his pants, leaned against the window and fell through. He and his parents claimed that the university should have posted warnings and provided proper supervision for dorm residents. The claim was denied. "We've got a kid that's presumably of average intelligence with his bare bottom against a window, leaning back," Al Campbell, claim manager for the state's Bureau of Risk Management Department, said. "That doesn't sound very bright to me."

FRAN FULTON, 47, WHO GAINED WEIGHT

while coping with a degenerative eye disease ("I found solace in food," she said), filed suit against Weight Watchers of Philadelphia, accusing the franchise of violating the Americans with Disabilities Act because it failed to provide audio tapes of its low-calorie recipes. As a result, she said she often strayed from her diet because her failing vision made it nearly impossible to read recipes or pamphlets explaining meals' nutritional components. Noting that she lost just 17 pounds under the program in eight months, Fulton insisted, "I think I should have lost 40 pounds."

DENNIS SMITH, 36, AN INMATE AT FLOR-
ida's Martin Correctional Institution, filed a lawsuit
against the state because he was denied estrogen,
which he said he needed to "match his physical appearance with his inner feelings." Smith, who goes by
the name Rhonda, said that he has had sex-change surgery, including breast implants, but needs hormone
treatments to remain a woman.

A GERMAN COUPLE WHO TOOK A CARIB-
bean cruise expecting to be serenaded by the sounds
of calypso music instead found themselves forced to
listen to Swiss yodelers for two weeks. Most of the 600
passengers were members of the Swiss Union of
Friends of Folk Music, who entertained themselves by
performing almost the entire time. Even the Latin
American midnight buffet was accompanied by a Swiss
brass band. On their return, the couple sued the tour
operator. The Frankfurt District Court ordered a re-
fund of one-third of their $4,478 fare.

CONVICTED ROBBER KENNETH D. PARKER
filed suit in U.S. District Court in Reno, Nevada, claiming that his civil rights and rights to property were

violated. He explained that while serving time at the state prison in Carson City, he ordered a jar of chunky peanut butter from the prison store. He was given creamy but rejected it. Parker said he was then transferred to the new state prison in Ely, but the chunky peanut butter never caught up with him. U.S. District Judge Edward C. Reed dismissed the case, noting that it already had cost several hundred dollars in court and lawyers' time. "Plaintiff is out one jar of crunchy peanut butter worth $2.50," the judge explained, "and should seek relief through the prison grievance system of the Nevada small-claims court."

ANTHONY YOKLEY, SERVING 10 YEARS for counterfeiting at the Federal Correctional Institution in Jefferson County, Colorado, appealed his sentence as unfair because it includes three leap years. He claimed that his punishment would be "impermissibly enhanced by three days in violation of his equal protection and due process rights." The 10th Circuit Court of Appeals ruled "that this novel argument is without merit."

A 31-YEAR-OLD PRISON INMATE IN PORT-land, Oregon, sued the state for refusing to provide him with dental floss, a policy which he said has caused him stress because he is powerless to fight tooth decay. Prison officials insisted that the floss can be used as a weapon or to "cut through bars."

ALSO IN PORTLAND, A 405-POUND, 36-year-old man sued Denny's Inc. for $1.3 million because he said his weight qualifies him as "disabled," and the restaurant could not accommodate his needs. The restaurant's failure to provide a booth or chair big enough to support him left him feeling like "a clown on parade."

A 37-YEAR-OLD WOMAN FILED A LAWSUIT against Splash Casino in Memphis, Tennessee, after her husband shot himself to death following his loss of $100,000 while gambling there. The woman charged that the casino should have noticed her husband could not control himself.

A NEW YORK CITY WOMAN SUED HER former psychiatrist for $5 million, charging that he seduced her into a sexual relationship. According to her testimony, when she asked him whether it was proper for them to be having sex, he "told me that when his medical class took the Hippocratic oath he was not present and it did not apply to him."

IN PHILADELPHIA, DORIS JACKSON FILED a lawsuit against the city for losing her son's brain. Thomas Seabron, 26, died in a motorcycle accident more than two years earlier. When Jackson went to the funeral home, she discovered that the morgue had removed her son's brain and wouldn't tell her its whereabouts.

AT BRITAIN'S WHITEMOOR PRISON, IN-mates Peter Sherry, Gilbert McNamee, Liam O'Dwyer and Liam McCotter filed a lawsuit seeking $80,500 each. They charged prison officials were negligent in treating injuries received while they were escaping from the high-security prison.

Injudicious Judges

LOS ANGELES SUPERIOR COURT JUDGE Edward Kakita fined the law firm of Spray, Gould & Bowers $2,500 for submitting legal briefs with one-and-a-half line spacing instead of two lines. A state appeals court reversed Kakita's ruling, explaining that federal law requires one-and-a-half line spacing, but state law mandates double spacing.

IN HOUSTON, THE ATTORNEY FOR DEATH row inmate Robert Nelson Drew complained when District Judge Charles J. Hearn signed Drew's execution order and then added a happy face to the document. Hearn said that the symbol was "not intended to take away from the seriousness of anything. It's just become part of my signature. My driver's license is signed that way."

IN THE PHILIPPINES, MANILA JUDGE MAX-imiano Asuncion recommended that people convicted of crimes carrying the death sentence be made to wrestle poisonous snakes inside a giant tank open to public view.

AFTER WEATHERSFIELD, CONNECTICUT, stockbroker Ralph Presutti, 53, was censured and suspended for two months by the New York Stock Exchange for insider trading, his lawyers complained to the Securities and Exchange Commission that the three-member disciplinary board "missed a major part of Mr. Presutti's defense because they were napping." The lawyers told the SEC that two of the panel members were observed sleeping no fewer than seven times over three days of hearings.

In Portsmouth, England, Terence
Hadenham, 44, was convicted of gross indecency and indecent assault on a six-year-old girl. Rather than sentence him to jail, Judge John Whitley fined Hadenham $75 and gave him three years probation, citing Hadenham's stunted growth and a hearing impairment that made it difficult for him to form relationships with women.

In Jonestown, Pennsylvania, District
Justice William E. Schadler dismissed speeding charges against model Vera Cox, 30, because her good looks made him believe her story that she was fleeing "four scruffy guys" who followed her from New Jersey. Schadler admitted that he wouldn't have believed Cox, who was ticketed for driving 122 mph, if she were "fat and ugly" or "an ugly broad."

The Arizona Commission on Judicial
Conduct reprimanded Magistrate Michael Lex for telling a woman prosecutor that "only whores wear red shoes." Brenda Cook, a Tucson assistant city prosecutor who filed the complaint, was wearing red shoes

when Lex made the remark, but Lex contended that he did not notice Cook's shoes but was referring generally to other people's reactions to red.

REDBOOK MAGAZINE NAMED ALLEGHENY County, Pennsylvania, Judge Robert P. Horgos one of "America's Most Sexist Judges" for asking a male attorney to take off his jacket, then inviting a female lawyer to "take off anything you want." Also named was Thomas Bollinger of Baltimore County, Maryland, who granted probation to a man convicted of raping a drunken woman, explaining that an unconscious woman on a bed was "the dream of a lot of males, quite honestly."

TENNESSEE CRIMINAL COURT JUDGE Doug Meyer ordered a rape suspect released despite a prosecutor's suggestion that he appoint a guardian for the suspect until a formal hearing. Meyer said, "I don't think he needs it, really. I think what he needs—he needs a girlfriend, because if he doesn't, he's going to have bad dreams again." Meyer, in the face of subsequent public complaints, ordered the suspect taken into custody three days later.

U.S. TAX COURT JUDGE JOAN SEITZ PATE

ruled that exotic dancer Cynthia S. Hess, known professionally as "Chesty Love," was entitled to claim a $2,088 deduction for depreciation on the surgical implants that enlarged her bust to 56FF. The Internal Revenue Service had rejected the deduction, explaining that expenses to enhance a taxpayer's appearance, while useful for business, are too personal to be a business expense. The judge ruled that the implants increased Hess's income and that she couldn't derive personal benefit from her breasts because "they were so large that they ruined her personal appearance, her health and imposed severe stress on her personal and family relationships."

AFTER HIS ELECTION TO THE HIGHEST

Texas court that hears criminal appeals, Steve Mansfield admitted to *Texas Lawyer* a host of campaign lies, among them his vast criminal-court experience (he is an insurance and tax lawyer), that he was born in Texas (Massachusetts) and that he dated a woman who died (she was still alive). Mansfield called these and other claims "puffery" and "exaggerations" and promised to stop now that he is one of the state's highest-ranking judges.

CHIEF JUSTICE WILLIAM REHNQUIST IN 1995 added four stripes on each sleeve of his robe, the first such adornment in Supreme Court history. Rehnquist explained that the idea came to him while watching Gilbert and Sullivan's comic opera *Iolanthe*, which pokes fun at, among other things, British courts.

SOURCES

Anchorage Times
Arizona Republic
Asahi Evening News (Tokyo)
Asheville Citizen (North Carolina)
Associated Press
Atlanta Constitution
Bangor Daily News (Maine)
Beacon Journal (Cleveland)
Bible Advocate
Boston Globe
Boston Herald
Brisbane Sunday Mail (Australia)
Buffalo News
Charlotte Observer
Chicago Tribune
Chicago Sun-Times
Columbia Journalism Review

Columbus Dispatch (Ohio)
Daily Mirror (U.K.)
Daily Telegraph (U.K.)
Daily News (California)
Dallas Morning News
Denver Post
Des Moines Register
Details
Detroit Free Press
Detroit News
Deutsche Presse-Agentur
The Economist
Entertainment Weekly
The European
Evening Sun (Baltimore)
Fortean Times
Fort Worth Star-Telegram
Glasgow Herald
Globe and Mail
Harper's
Houston Post
The Independent (U.K.)
International Herald Tribune
Johannesburg Star
Journal (Knoxville)
Journal (Milwaukee)
Journal of Commerce
Kansas City Star
Key West Citizen (Florida)
Knoxville News-Sentinel (Tennessee)
Lincoln Journal-Star (Nebraska)
London Times
Los Angeles Times
Miami Herald

Minneapolis Star Tribune
Morning Call (Allentown, Pennsylvania)
Nashville Banner (Tennessee)
New Haven Register
New Scientist
New York Daily News
New York Newsday
New York Post
New York Times
Newsweek
Olympian (Olympia, Washington)
Orange County Register (California)
Oregonian
Parade
People
Philadelphia Daily News
Philadelphia Inquirer
Plain Dealer (Cleveland)
Pocono Record
Post-Standard (Syracuse, New York)
Press Democrat (Santa Rosa, California)
Press-Sun Bulletin (Binghamton, New York)
Raleigh News & Observer (North Carolina)
Record-Journal (Meriden, Connecticut)
Reuters
Rocky Mountain News
Roll Call
Saint Paul Pioneer Press
St. Louis Post-Dispatch
Saginaw News (Michigan)
Salt Lake Tribune
San Francisco Chronicle
San Francisco Examiner
San Jose Mercury News (California)

Scranton Times
Scripps-Howard
Seattle Post-Intelligencer
Seattle Times
Shreveport Times
Southeast Missourian (Cape Girardeau)
Star-Ledger (Newark, New Jersey)
Stars and Stripes
Strange
Sydney Morning Herald
Syracuse Herald-Journal (New York)
Sun (Baltimore)
Sunday Times (Scranton, Pennsylvania)
Tampa Tribune
Tennessean (Nashville)
Texas Monthly
Times-Leader (Wilkes-Barre, Pennsylvania)
Times-Picayune (New Orleans)
Time
Today London
Toronto Sun (Ontario)
Tribune (Scranton, Pennsylvania)
United Press International
USA Today
Waco Tribune Herald (Texas)
Wall Street Journal
Washington Post
Washington Times
Wellington Evening Post (New Zealand)
World Press Review